SPAIN'S HIDDEN COUNTRY

A Traveller's Guide to Northern Spain

SPAIN'S HIDDEN COUNTRY

A TRAVELLER'S GUIDE TO NORTHERN SPAIN

Frank Barrett

and

Chris Gill

Published by
Telegraph Publications
in association with
Brittany Ferries

Published by Telegraph Publications
135 Fleet Street, London EC4P 4BL

First published 1986
Second edition 1987

Designed by Fox + Partners, Bath
Cover illustration by Murray Zanoni
Other illustrations by Eileen Knight, Bristol
Maps by David Perrott, Machynlleth
Typeset by Fox + Partners and Wordsmiths, London
Printed in Great Britain by Biddles Ltd, Guildford

ISBN 0 86367 069 5

CONTENTS

ACKNOWLEDGMENTS

A word about our sponsors and our many helpers

This is the second edition of *Spain's Hidden Country*, thoroughly updated to take account of the changes that have taken place since the first edition was published early in 1986. The new cover illustration is one of a series done by the artist Murray Zanoni for Wines of Spain, and appears with their kind permission.

Our thanks are due to Brittany Ferries, who took us to Northern Spain and arranged our accommodation there. Without their help, the cost of researching a book of this kind would have made the whole project uneconomic. We are grateful to have had the comments of some key members of Brittany Ferries' staff on the draft of the book; but the judgments the book contains are those of ourselves and our fellow researchers.

Particular thanks are due to the many holidaymakers who helped us by filling in our questionnaire about Northern Spain on their way home with Brittany Ferries, and to those readers of the first edition who answered our call for further help; the quotes you will find throughout the book reflect what these two groups have told us. The intention is to revise the guide annually, so if you take this edition to Spain please do let us have feedback on what you find; at the back of the book on page 156 we suggest the sort of information we really need.

Frank Barrett
Chris Gill

Bath
January 1987

About This Book

The key to a holiday you'll treasure for ever

They were a retired couple in their early seventies, from Torquay. We met them in the hotel bar: over an evening sherry they were scribbling off closely written postcards chronicling their memorable journey along the Pilgrims' Way through Burgos to Santiago.

They were full of excitement over their holiday in Northern Spain, which was all that they had hoped and more. From their reading at home they knew all about the area's history and culture; they knew which were the sights to see, and where were the places to stay. They had managed to learn some Spanish at evening classes. From people who knew the region they had learnt which roads to avoid, and how much ground to aim to cover. In short, they had been thoroughly prepared for their trip, and as a result they were thoroughly enjoying it.

A few evenings later, in the mountains beyond León, we met another retired couple in another hotel bar. They were sitting miserably nursing what looked like a very stiff drink, clearly attempting to drown their sorrows.

They had decided to go to Northern Spain rather on the spur of the moment: only days after the brochure had caught their eye on a travel agent's shelf, they had driven off the ferry at Santander having almost no idea of what to expect or where they wanted to go – and after a too-long day on the road had ended up in a 'flea-pit' hotel. Now, a day later, they were still completely fed up, and regretting the whole idea. Happily, the British contingent in the bar were quick to rally round: maps were produced, guide-books were consulted, and a suggested itinerary was drawn up for them. Later on we found them in a much more cheerful and contented state of mind, enthusiastically looking forward to the next day's travels.

The lesson is clear. Northern Spain has one great advantage over other areas which can match its scenery, heritage, beaches and hotels: it is just about the only place left in southern Europe where you can go as a traveller in a foreign land and not as a tourist progressing from one well-known 'attraction' to the next. But being off the beaten tourist track means that you have to find your own way, literally and metaphorically: the highlights are widely spread, and easily missed unless you know what you're about. Hardly anybody speaks English, even in the most popular areas, and in out-of-the-way places you may be the only foreigner in town – so it helps if you're a bit of an adventurer, and if you speak a bit of Spanish.

What you need most of all is information and guidance – clear pointers to which places are most worth aiming for, and why. And that's what this book provides. It does not catalogue every Romanesque chapel and every wayside hotel – on the contrary, we have aimed to be highly selective, so that the job of deciding where to go and where to stay becomes as simple as possible.

Most of the information is organised around 'bases' – cities, towns, and villages which are worth staying in at least for a night. Many of our bases are attractive in themselves, or have interesting sights to see. But we haven't stopped at that: any itinerary should take account of the sprinkling of exceptional hotels in the area (many of them members of the state-run Parador chain) – so some of our bases are included because they possess such a hotel. Every base gets the same thorough treatment, with descriptions of worthwhile excursions in the surrounding countryside as well as details of the sights and hotels in the place itself.

Spain's Hidden Country is the first practical, all-in-one 'user's guide' to Northern Spain. We hope that its publication will encourage many more people to visit the area to see for themselves its unique attractions. Those who are already addicted to its charms may see a guide like this as a threat to the area's status as a sort of tourist-free zone. We don't think they need worry. Northern Spain may have the beaches to become a mass-market tourism destination – better beaches, in fact, than anything on the Costa del Sol in the south – but it doesn't have the weather. The weather can be hot – much hotter in places than Britain; but it is an Atlantic coast, and the climate is neither as warm nor as predictable as that of the Mediterranean. The package holidaymakers will continue to head south. San Sebastián will never be another Benidorm.

The north is a region for those who enjoy travelling – those who take pleasure in magnificent scenery, exceptional architecture and superb hotels, and who are content to adapt to a relaxed way of life very different from their own. They will never come here in millions. Happily, it's a secret which we can afford to share.

Introduction

What makes Northern Spain different – in a nutshell

Some foreign countries are familiar even to those who have never set foot within their borders. The first-time traveller to France, for example, is in for precious few surprises – the history of France, its culture and way of life have run closely together with those of Britain for almost 1,000 years; the French language is widely taught at school; from the TV and cinema we build up a fairly detailed knowledge of everyday life across the Channel almost without realising it.

We are quite familiar with the accomplishments of the French: they're people who create and enjoy good food and wine, famous as lovers and celebrated as artists. But what of the Spanish? Their single notable contribution to the culinary canon is *paella*; as for art, perhaps Picasso was Spanish – or was he French? Few British schoolchildren learn Spanish, and few British people have any real inkling of the Spanish way of life; we know next to nothing of their rich history, their religious struggle, their period of world domination, their contribution to art and literature.

Spain might be the most popular foreign holiday destination for the British, but few can claim any real knowledge of the country. Like the D-Day army, the invasion has been bottled up around the beaches, with only the boldest making progress inland. Spain is mainly known to the British as a land of sun and sand, cheap booze, castanets, flamenco dancers, gipsy guitarists, bull-fights and incompetent waiters called Manuel. Historically, all we know of Spain is that our chaps gave them a sound beating when Drake finished his game of bowls before going out to polish off the Armada.

If we know little of Spain as a whole, we know next to nothing about Northern Spain – even for the citizens of central and southern Spain, the north is something of a closed book. If we hear anything about the area, it is of the Basque country and the separatist group ETA, which has pursued its aims with bombings and assassinations. But this is like thinking of Britain only in terms of the IRA. For the traveller driving through Northern Spain, this internal struggle is evident only in the paint-obliterated road-signs, where non-Basque spellings are blocked out.

But it is our very lack of familiarity with Northern Spain that makes a visit there such an exciting prospect. Visiting France for the first time is a confirmation of what you already half-expected. Landing in Northern Spain for the first time is by comparison a thrilling leap into the unknown.

There are all sorts of rewards for making the leap. There is spectacular mountain scenery in the Picos de Europa, while a couple of hundred miles to the west, in contrast, are the subtle wooded coastlines of Galicia. There are magnificent buildings: the cathedrals of Santiago de Compostela and León are among the finest of their kind in the world; the narrow cobbled streets of Santillana del Mar and Pontevedra are still to be found much as they were 300 years ago, each house with its patrician coat of arms and each with its wrought iron balcony garlanded with flowers. Along the 875km coast-road from Irún to Vigo, there are dozens and dozens of wide, soft, sandy beaches, many of them deserted of visitors even at the height of the season. Equally there are elegant, cosmopolitan resorts like San Sebastián. Among the hotels in Northern Spain are two of the world's finest: Los Reyes Catolicos in Santiago, and the San Marcos in León. There are also more than a dozen Paradores, reliable state-run hotels, many of them set in handsome, historic buildings or with outstanding views.

But the supreme attraction of Northern Spain is that it has so far evaded the attentions of the mass-market tourism business. With the exception of Santiago, which can claim to be the world's oldest tourist trap, you'll have trouble finding a genuine souvenir shop anywhere in Northern Spain. If the local folk dress up in their regional costume and dance to the sound of the Galician bagpipes or to the beat of the Cantabrian drum, they'll be doing so for their own and their fellows' amusement, not for some ersatz folkloric spectacular.

Northern Spain will surprise you, perhaps even shock you. It's only a day's travel from Britain, yet in the rural areas life is rooted almost in the Middle Ages. On the roads every few miles you will pass carts pulled by donkeys or teams of bullocks; in the fields, you will see the grass cut by scythe as it has been for centuries, and nearly always the scythes will be wielded by old men and women. The fields are not the giant, uniformly farmed areas we have become used to in Britain; they are narrow strips, each one the property of a different local resident. Weedkillers and crop sprays have not so far wiped out the mass of wild flowers which carpet the grassy fields, and which attract masses of brightly coloured butterflies.

And if the people's way of life is old-fashioned, so is their politeness and the good-heartedness of their welcome; a touch formal, perhaps, but most agreeable. There is nothing here of the impression you get in some other places – that tourists are seen only as units of a mega-dollar industry, ripe for exploitation or simply mugging.

In most places in Northern Spain tourists are still enough of a curiosity to warrant special treatment. In La Coruña we were stopped in the street by a lady who overheard us talking: 'English?' she asked. 'If you need any help or assistance at any time, this is my telephone number – don't hesitate to call.' While the modern pace of Britain has created a nation of introverts, almost desperate not to get 'involved' with anyone else, Northern Spain is still very much a society of people, keen to invite friendship and share hospitality.

The difference seems to be that the people of Northern Spain, even those who live in the jumble of tower-block flats that sprout up like forests around the cities of the north-east, are essentially people of the countryside. Unlike the city dwellers of Britain, the urban Spanish have never entirely lost their links with the land. They take their pleasures in food and drink, they like to meet and talk, and above all there is nothing they enjoy more than a *fiesta*, with its singing, dancing and carousing.

Spain as a whole was for centuries isolated from the mainstream of European life – partly because of its geographical separateness, as a peninsula cut off by the natural barrier of the Pyrenees. While Britain was at the height of its powers in the industrial revolution, Spain was a poverty-stricken peasant economy (it began its industrial revolution only in this century). When the whole of Europe was furiously engaged in World War I, Spain's separateness is highlighted by the fact that it played no part. (While towns and cities in other European countries are chockablock with memorials to the dead of the World Wars, there are no such monuments in Spain – only occasional reminders of the glorious struggle against the Bonapartist armies of the French in the first decade of the 19th century.) Even Spain's private war – the appalling Civil War of the 1930s – contributed to the country's continuing isolation, bringing the dictator Franco to power and thus plunging Spain into a new political wilderness.

But now, after 400 years of isolation and stagnation, Spain is clearly on the way back, gearing up to exploit its membership of the Common Market. Those who drive through the north and north-east will see ample evidence of the increasing industrialisation.

Factory follows factory, with steel-works and chemical works belching smoke and fumes, as they used to in the heavy industrial areas of Britain. But amongst the smoking chimneys and the spiralling web of motorways and flyovers, there are still the fields with their curious Christmas-pudding haystacks, supervised by bronzed old men in black berets.

Spain is clearly going to change; the prosperity brought by tourism has already changed much of southern Spain out of all recognition. So far, Northern Spain has not been affected. The strong provincial life of areas like Galicia and the Basque country will ensure that it will not easily give up its traditions. But it is difficult to see how the attractive easy-going life of Northern Spain can remain completely unchanged following entry into the EEC.

The land beyond the mountains

By Northern Spain we mean a strip of country running across the northern coast, its southern boundary more-or-less coinciding with the northern limit of Portugal. The coastal regions of the Basque country, Cantabria, Asturias and Galicia are at the heart of Spain's 'hidden country', north of the mountains of the Cordillera Cantabrica; but we have also covered the countryside and cities within easy reach of the coast, in the regions of Navarra and La Rioja, and major cities of tourist interest in the north of Castilla-León – León itself, and Burgos.

This is a relatively small part of the Iberian peninsula, but its dimensions are nevertheless impressive. From Cabo Fisterra (the western extremity of Spain as a whole, as well as the limit of our area) to the French border at Irun is 600km as the crow flies – about as far as from London to the middle of Scotland. Our strip measures 200km from north to south at its widest point.

It surprises many visitors that Spain is such a mountainous country – as a whole it's the second most mountainous in Europe, after Switzerland, and Northern Spain has more than its share of high ground and peaks. Running west from the Pyrenees is another mighty range of mountains: the Cordillera Cantabrica, which stretches almost the whole way across the northern coast of Spain. This range reaches its highest point at over 2600 metres in the spectacular Picos de Europa, which lie about 30km inland from the coast between Santander and Oviedo. Just as the Pyrenees blocked communication between Spain and France, so has this line of mountains succeeded in dividing Northern Spain from the rest of the country. While Spain was invaded by a succession of armies including the Romans and the Moors, the land beyond these mountains remained free, safely sheltered from attack.

This is Spain's 'hidden country'. The provinces which lie behind and among these mountains take pride in their effective geographical isolation from the rest of the Spain. The fierce local pride of the inhabitants, characterised at its most extreme by those Basques who wish to break away from Spain altogether, can be explained by this sense of 'separateness' which the mountains have served to create.

Northern Spain – or at least, the part of it north of the mountains – has quite a different climate from the high plains to the south – generally cooler and wetter. The vegetation is lusher, the trees greener and the fields appear to be more productive. The coastline is buffeted by the restless Atlantic; following the coast road, you come across beach after beach – almost every one a deserted expanse of pale sand washed by huge breakers. It is a Spain that would be recognised by few holidaymakers familiar with the burnt *sierras* and arid *mesetas* of the south. The lushness and the green-ness of the countryside, and its indented *rías*, make the area reminiscent of Cornwall, Brittany or Ireland. When you ask British people why they are so fond of Northern Spain, and why they return here year after year, many say it is because the region is 'so much like home'.

Within this northern strip beyond the mountains, there are contrasts almost equally profound. In many eastern and in some central parts – around Bilbao, for example, and Oviedo – there is heavy industry on a huge scale, while to the west in Galicia the economy appears to be sustained almost wholly on fishing and agriculture. But Galicia is different in many respects from the rest of Northern Spain – geographically (it is not so dramatically mountainous); culturally (it has a Celtic background, principally revealed nowadays in its passion for bagpipes!); and climatically (it has a much milder climate than elsewhere in the North).

Away from the factory chimneys of Bilbao, or the coal-mines and steel-works of the Asturias, it is a region of astonishingly beautiful countryside. Each day's driving will take you up breathtaking mountain passes, through beautiful valleys, beside delightful lakes or among marvellously scented pine and eucalyptus forests. The scenery changes almost with each turn of the road. It is difficult to imagine any area of this size offering more variety of land- and sea-scape.

Many travellers to the area remember the scenery as the highlight of the trip; some typical comments from holidaymakers' questionnaires:

'Breathtaking and beautiful ... the scenery and the empty sandy beaches are of great beauty' Mr and Mrs Burrows.
'Beautiful green fields, mountains and hills resembling England, and after two and a half years living in Gibraltar – a welcome sight!' Penny and Sean O'Callaghan
'Fantastic scenery' John Hallett
'Mountain scenery beautiful – it's almost English!' Mr and Mrs Ashmore
'Varied scenery and lush vegetation' Mr and Mrs Barnikel

711 AND ALL THAT

A concise history, to illuminate your travels

To get the most out of your visit to Northern Spain, it really does help to have some grasp of Spanish history. If you know the key historical events, you can make much more sense of the places and historic monuments you will see during your travels.

The invasion of the Moors

For most of us, English history begins in 1066 with the Battle of Hastings and the Norman invasion. Of course, important events such as the Roman invasion and the arrival of the Norsemen and the Anglo-Saxons happened before then, but after the happenings of 1066 Britain took on a different identity, and a much more significant role in world affairs.

For Spain, the key year was unquestionably 711, when the Moors invaded from North Africa. While Britain was still in that historical period known as the Dark Ages, the Arabs were culturally at a much more advanced stage. With their invasion they brought a storehouse of knowledge on a wide range of subjects – everything from architecture to astronomy. Spain, and Europe as a whole, clearly stood to benefit from the Muslim culture. Not surprisingly, this isn't how the Spanish saw things; they remained devout Christians. But they were quite unable to resist the mighty Moorish advance, which swept through the Spanish peninsula and on into the heart of France, only coming to a halt at Poitiers.

Until 722 Christianity seemed doomed. But in that year there occurred an event which was to be a turning point in Spain's history – and it happened at the very heart of Northern Spain, at Covadonga, in a valley among the Picos de Europa. A force of Muslim soldiers sent to deal with local resistance were attacked and killed by an army led by a tribal leader called Pelayo. Never before had the Muslims been fought and beaten; suddenly, their invincibility was questioned. The small success of Pelayo, who thus became the first King of Spain, acted as a focal point for the resistance against the invading Moors.

The fight to recover Spain from the Moors, known as the Reconquest (*la Reconquista*), was a marathon effort accomplished piece by piece over no less than 781 years: it wasn't until Granada was recaptured in 1492 that the Muslims were finally beaten and eventually expelled.

As the Moors never managed to conquer the whole north of Spain, their presence isn't as clearly visible as it is in the south, where you can see their finest works such as the Alhambra in Granada or the mosque in Cordoba. The importance of the Arab occupation for the north lies in the Christian religious zeal which it generated. The cult of St James at Santiago and the profusion of cathedrals, churches and monasteries throughout the area clearly owe much to the feelings generated by the Reconquest. This Christian zealotry ultimately had less pleasant effects in the shape of the Spanish Inquisition – an appalling and protracted persecution of Protestants, Jews and Moors initiated in the 15th century, when it was managed by the notorious Inquisitor General Torquemada. Those suspected of 'heresy' were cruelly tortured and subsequently burnt.

El Camino de Santiago (The Way of Saint James)

In the Middle Ages, Northern Spain held a supremely important place in European life, as it lay in the path of pilgrims to the shrine of Saint James in Santiago de Compostela (see page 51 for a complete account of the legend). By the time of the Battle of Hastings, Santiago had become a place of pilgrimage almost as important as Rome and Jerusalem; as Santiago was much easier to get to than Rome for most Europeans – and since Jerusalem eventually fell into the hands of the Muslims – Santiago became the most visited city in Europe. It certainly became the first foreign place that people travelled to on a large scale for reasons other than war or commerce. Its popularity with the British can be judged by the fact that one of Chaucer's Canterbury Pilgrims, the Wife of Bath, claimed to have made the pilgrimage. No doubt she decided to forgo the lengthy trek taken by the truly devout pilgrims through France and across Northern Spain, and instead opted for the more leisurely route of sailing to La Coruña or Vigo and travelling the short distance across country.

Santiago's pre-eminence, which lasted until well into the 16th century, dramatically altered the face of Northern Spain's towns and cities. The major places which lay on the Pilgrims' Way – such as Burgos, León and Lugo – became prosperous, boasting elegant buildings and magnificent cathedrals. Castles such as the one at Ponferrada were built to accommodate the Knights Templar, whose job it was to protect pilgrims; superb hospitals and hospices were erected (such as the Hostal San Marcos in León and Hotel de Los Reyes Católicos in Santiago) to care for sick and weary pilgrims.

The religious fervour generated by the pilgrimage inspired the architects of the time to produce their finest work, particularly in the style which came to be called Plateresque (see the end of this chapter for an explanation). The apex of the pilgrimage-inspired architecture is undoubtedly the cathedral at Santiago, but those who travel along the Way of Saint James to this great city will find hundreds of buildings along the way which were constructed at the height of the pilgrimage and are still perfectly intact.

The Golden Age

In the same year – 1492 – that the Spanish, led by the Catholic Monarchs (Los Reyes Católicos) Ferdinand and Isabella, recaptured Granada and completed the Reconquest, an equally significant event was happening across the Atlantic: Columbus was discovering America. In 1519, when Cortés captured Mexico and treasure ships laden with gold and silver began to return to ports in Northern Spain such as Bayona and La Coruña, Spain was consolidating its position as the dominant world power. Through becoming Holy Roman Emperor, the King of Spain added Germany, Austria, Holland and Belgium to the existing Spanish possessions of Naples, Sicily and Sardinia.

In 1588 Philip II assembled his Armada to attack England. Its objectives were three-fold; to revenge the execution of staunch Catholic Mary, Queen of Scots; to press his own claim to the English throne; and to prevent Queen Elizabeth from offering further support to the Protestants who were waging war against Spain in the Low Countries. The subsequent disasters which overtook the Armada effectively marked the beginning of the end of Spain as a major world power.

The Peninsular War

Over the next 200 years Spanish fortunes declined considerably, thanks to a combination of weak monarchs and a series of debilitating wars. By 1808 Spain had fallen under the control of the French Emperor Napoleon – the Spanish navy was largely destroyed by Nelson at the Battle of Trafalgar. But when Napoleon attempted to instal his brother Joseph as King of Spain, the Spanish people rebelled and began a war of independence which became the Peninsular War. The Allied fight against Napoleon was led by Sir Arthur Wellesley (afterwards Duke of Wellington) and the French general Suchet. The war ended with Napoleon's abdication in 1814.

The Civil War

Over the next 100 years, Spain was plagued by a succession of internal wars and uprisings which continued to divide the country and helped isolate it from the profound social and economic changes which were taking place in the rest of Europe. Spain's continuing constitutional crises reached their height in the early 1930s, when a socialist republican government took power and the king went into exile. The socialist plans for provincial autonomy, land reform and measures to limit the power of the Church were opposed by a new right wing party. Catalonia decided to become autonomous and there were violent insurrections in the Asturian capital of Oviedo.

Civil War eventually became inevitable, breaking out in the summer of 1936. Like our own English Civil War, it was the most brutal and bloody of wars. The Nationalists led by General Franco fought a bitter and violent struggle with the Republicans, in a war which lasted almost three years. The image which many of us have of the Civil War is Picasso's famous painting 'Guernica' which captured the agony and suffering of the period. Guernica, a small town near Bilbao, was bombed on a market day in April 1937 by a squadron of German aircraft, killing over 2,000 people in little more than three hours.

Franco eventually triumphed at the end of March, 1939. The country he took control of was almost a wasteland. Starved of money and raw materials it faced an almost impossible job of trying to rebuild – particularly as it was ignored by much of the international community. It wasn't until 1955, for example, that the country was admitted into the United Nations.

Spain after Franco

Since the restoration of full democracy after the death of Franco in 1975, Spain has undergone some sweeping social changes. There are much wider personal freedoms, there is greater prosperity, regional autonomy has been introduced. Perhaps not all the changes have been entirely for the better. Less authoritarian state control has resulted in a greater degree of lawlessness: drug addiction has become more widespread – and in order to finance their drug-taking, addicts have preyed upon visiting tourists, robbing people in the street and stealing from cars. But it is clear that Spain is a much happier, more contented place since the passing of Franco. And with its entry to the EEC, the country is looking optimistically to the future to play a fuller part in the life of Europe; something which it has been effectively denied for nearly 200 years.

Historic buildings

Most towns and cities in Northern Spain sprawl outwards to the countryside in an untidy and apparently haphazard fashion; town planning – or planning approval of any sort – is a concept that seems to have eluded modern Spain. On the other hand, the centres of those towns and cities remain much as they have done for hundreds of years. All the various architectural styles – and the buildings produced by those styles – stand preserved as if in some large-scale museum. Take the Galician town of Pontevedra, for example; wandering around its extraordinarily well preserved old streets, it's easy to imagine yourself transported back several hundred years (or it would be easy if it weren't for the mopeds racing around like refugees from 'Easy Rider').

Every church, cathedral, castle and monastery on your itinerary – and many of the hotels – will have a different and complex history and will represent a different blend of architectural styles as a result. If you study the leaflets and listen to the guides, you'll probably recognise some of the the terms used to describe these styles and their creators; others won't be at all familiar. The basic set of terms isn't difficult to grasp – in no time at all, you'll find yourself casting an eye over every building you encounter and casually remarking to all and sundry: 'Romanesque, I would say, with some interesting Plateresque features ...'.

For the most part, Northern Spain was never occupied by the Moors, so you will not find architectural flights of fancy such as the Alhambra in Granada, or the mosque in Cordoba. Instead the area developed its own simple, workmanlike designs for its churches. Typical of this style – called pre-Romanesque and dating from the 8th to 11th centuries – are a number of Asturian churches in the Oviedo area, such as Santa Maria de Naranco and San Miguel de Lillo, which are all the more attractive for their simplicity of design and decoration.

While Christianity fought the Muslim faith, Christians themselves could not fail to be influenced by Arab style. Mozarabs were Christians living under Moorish rule who adopted the architectural style of the Arabs in the building of Christian churches. When the Arabs began to persecute Christians in the 9th century, the Mozarabs moved north and built their distinctive churches (a classic feature is the horse-shoe arch), many of which are to be seen throughout Northern Spain.

The style of architecture to be seen most frequently in the churches and cathedrals of Northern Spain is Romanesque. The rise of Santiago de Compostela in the 11th century as a destination for thousand upon thousand of pilgrims inspired a rash of building, most of which was in the Romanesque style – characterised by rounded barrel vaults and round arches, with doorways often elaborately sculptured. (Perhaps the best Romanesque work of all is Santiago cathedral itself, particularly the magnificent Portico de la Gloria, now enclosed within a much later Baroque façade).

The Gothic style, although widely followed in the rest of Europe from the 13th to the 16th century, failed to make much impact in Spain. Northern Spain, which had a particular fondness for simplicity of design and style, seems to have been particularly unenthusiastic about this new departure in architecture, with its soaring buttresses and extravagant stained glass. León's cathedral, however, is a classic work in the Gothic style.

Following the Reconquest and the unification of Spain in the 16th century, public buildings took on a much more exuberant tone. This period saw the emergence of the style known as Plateresque – so-called because the stonework (such as that to be seen on the San Marcos Hostal in León) was so finely carved that it resembled the work of silversmiths rather than anything previously produced by a mason with a chisel. The later part of this period saw the appearance of extravagantly ornate Baroque design – the high-point of Baroque is surely the façade of Santiago Cathedral which adorns the main square.

Bed and Board

What to expect in Northern Spain's hotels and restaurants

Northern Spain is certainly well blessed with spectacular scenery and fine historical sights. But even with all its undoubted attractions few people would be tempted to travel there unless there were equally good places to stay. Happily, there are: Northern Spain has some of the best hotels in Europe; and with its Paradores it can boast some of the finest-looking, best-situated, best-value hotels of any area in the world.

At the start it ought to be stressed that if you plan to travel to Northern Spain in search of the sort of tower-block resort hotel that has become typical of the holiday costas to the south, you will be disappointed. There are no children's clubs, no video lounges, no discothèques, no baby-minding services. The hotel restaurants make few concessions to people who don't speak Spanish (even those menus supposedly translated into English are hardly more intelligible than in the original Spanish) and there are no allowances for foreign tastes. At 9pm when most Anglo-Saxons are fondly looking forward to climbing the wooden hill to Bedfordshire, the Spanish open the dining rooms for dinner. Lunch starts at 1pm (at the very earliest) and continues until 4pm. It is all uncompromisingly Spanish. But as one couple we met remarked: 'If we'd wanted something like Torquay, then we'd have gone to Torquay.'

Crême de la crême

Heading the First Division of Northern Spain's hotels are undoubtedly the Hostal Los Reyes Católicos in Santiago and the Hostal San Marcos in León – both now part of the Parador chain, although they are still distinguished from your run-of-the-mill

Paradores. Both hotels were formerly medieval hospices and hospitals, built for the care of travellers on the Pilgrims' Way. They are magnificent buildings, with superb Plateresque exteriors and richly furnished interiors. We have heard occasional complaints about the off-handedness of service at both hotels. Certainly we never encountered it, and even if we had, it would hardly have diminished the experience of staying at either hotel. If you're planning a honeymoon (or a second, third or fourth honeymoon!) book yourself a week at each establishment – it would be difficult to make a more perfect start to a marriage.

Close on the heels of the top two comes the Hotel de la Reconquista in Oviedo. Not an original ancient monument (it was rebuilt on the site of a pilgrims' hospital, in the style of the original building), it nevertheless manages to capture much of the splendour and elegance of its two eminent rivals. The staff are cheerful and very helpful; the hotel is sumptuously furnished and decorated with excellent paintings by local artists.

Paradores

One of the highlights of a visit to Northern Spain is unquestionably the chain of Parador hotels. Paradores are state-run hotels, established in the 1920s to provide good accommodation where it was lacking. 'Parador' in Spanish means literally a 'stopping place' – a rather inelegant name, you might have thought, for what are frequently quite magnificent establishments where you are offered an experience rather more marvellous than merely 'stopping off' en route to somewhere else. There are now more than 80 Paradores, sprinkled all over Spain, and more than a third of them are to be found in castles, former convents and other ancient monuments or places of historic interest. Read some of the entries later in the book, and you'll see what this means – in more than one case, living in a medieval castle or palace in the centre of an historic town.

Many Paradores are to be found in places of outstanding natural beauty. Some are sumptuously furnished with tapestries, antique furniture and period paintings, and virtually all are decorated and furnished in traditional style – even if newly built. You can expect the bedrooms to be comfortably furnished and spacious, with big baths and giant bath-towels to match. Many Paradores now have mini-bars and direct-dial telephones in the rooms.

This is not to say that Paradores are perfect – far from it. They share to the full the weaknesses of Spanish hotel-keeping in general, which are perhaps explained by the famous Spanish tendency never to do today what can be put off until tomorrow.

For reasons which escape us, most Parador reception desks appear to be manned by the Spanish equivalent of Chelsea pensioners. Few receptionists, elderly or not, speak English, which seems curious since the majority of Parador guests speak little else. Arrangements for humping luggage to your bedroom are also erratic, hingeing as they often do on the abilities and disposition of the same elderly gentlemen. There are simple remedies to these problems: master some elementary Spanish, and don't always expect anybody to leap out to carry your luggage up to your room.

Simple problems of cleaning and maintenance also seem to fox the management of many Paradores; anything shiny will be polished daily, but carpets are expected to stay clean without the aid of vacuum cleaners; repairs to bedroom furniture are put off until they're unavoidable, and light bulbs don't get changed very often – and there appears to be a deep-seated reluctance to get the hot water system cranked up into action much before 8am. Again, these aren't major problems, but they may take you a little by surprise at first.

As elsewhere in Spain, the beds are always single, never double. The Pope probably approves, but there can be few other people who are happy with this state of affairs. It ought to be fairly widely appreciated these days that not even single people want single beds. And the Parador beds are slightly narrower than even the normal single dimensions so that you're only really comfortable when you're lying on your side – one false move and you can end up impaled on the bedside light.

But let's not be too churlish. After all, the majority of Paradores are of only three-star standard, so you can't expect a five-star standard of attention to detail; by the same token, you're not paying five-star prices. Paradores are clearly good value for money. Even the most expensive Parador is nowhere near as expensive as the better city-centre hotels in Bilbao or Pamplona, for example, or the Crême de la crême hotels picked out above. Another merit is that they operate to a reasonably consistent standard – you know if you book into a Parador that, whatever the imperfections, you'll be reasonably comfortable and adequately fed.

Although they are of a fairly even standard of comfort it is true to say that certain Paradores in Northern Spain are more attractive than others. Taking account of both the buildings themselves and their settings, this is our Top Eight (nominations welcome for two more to make it Ten!); they're in alphabetical order – for more detailed information about each one, see the relevant 'base' entry:

Bayona
Fuenterrabía
Olite
Pontevedra
Ribadeo
Santillana del Mar
Verín
Villalba

Other hotels

In most of our 'base' entries we've picked out a single hotel (usually the local Parador, or one of the other remarkable hotels described above) as our recommendation – and sometimes we've said that there's little point in going there unless you're going to stay in that hotel. But many towns are worth visiting even if you can't get into the outstanding hotel in the area, so we have normally described alternatives to our main recommendation; these hotels are rarely especially captivating, but are perfectly adequate and good value. In some places there is no outstanding hotel, in which case we have simply described the options open to you.

There are cheaper hotels than Paradores, there are bed and breakfast places, and there are also camp-sites – all of which may be entirely satisfactory. But the special attraction of Northern Spain is its Paradores and other grand hotels; if you don't use them fairly frequently, you'll be missing quite a lot of the fun of the place as a holiday destination.

Booking ahead

As far as your accommodation is concerned, planning is absolutely of the essence. It is possible to go without any pre-booked accommodation and travel around taking pot luck. But it is not wise, even out of the peak season. The most popular Paradores, such as those at Bayona, Fuenterrabía, Pontevedra, Ribadeo and Santillana del Mar, are very heavily booked (Santillana del Mar is within an hour's drive of the ferry at Santander, so the perfect place to spend the last night of the holiday). If you don't book ahead, you're very likely to be disappointed. Similarly, booking is essential at the San Marcos in León, Los Reyes Católicos in Santiago and the Hotel de la Reconquista in Oviedo.

If you don't feel like committing yourself to hotel bookings for the whole of your trip, it would still be a good idea to make reservations for these top hotels and take a chance on other nights. If you are travelling on an inclusive package with Brittany Ferries, you will make your reservations through the ferry company and receive vouchers. Similarly if you are booking a fly-drive package, the hotel reservations will be be handled by the tour operator. If you are planning to travel independently, you can make reservations through a London agency, Keytel, which handles bookings not only for Paradores but also for a variety of other Spanish hotel groups. You pay Keytel before departure and they will issue the necessary vouchers. You could, of course, book with the relevant hotel direct, if your Spanish is up to it.

Food

Spanish cooking, like Spanish culture in general, varies a lot from region to region; but if you have been to other parts of Spain, some of what you'll find in Northern Spain will be familiar. The classic Spanish dish in the minds of foreigners is *paella* – saffron-flavoured rice plus more-or-less anything else which comes to hand, particularly seafood – and although it originates in Valencia, at the other end of the country, it does appear on northern menus. As elsewhere in coastal Spain, seafood stews are a staple, whether known as *bullabesa* (in content as well as name similar to the *bouillabaisse* of southern France), *zarzuela de mariscos*, *calderata Asturiana* (in Asturias) or whatever.

Fish and other seafood are naturally very common throughout the north, from the scallops for which Galicia is famous to the *merluza* (hake) and *bacalao* (cod) which are rarely missing from menus in the Basque country – characteristic local dishes include *merluza a la Bilbaína* (hake fried in egg and flour) and *bacalao a la Viscaína* (cod baked in an onion, tomato and red pepper sauce). The Basque country is known as the gastronomic headquarters of Spain – though this isn't necessarily obvious to the visitor, particularly if you stick to eating in hotels. Its reputation is partly supported by the many good restaurants in cities such as Bilbao and San Sebastián, but probably owes more to the famous gastronomic societies – men-only affairs apparently devoted to furthering the culinary arts. Asturias has its share of fish dishes, but is better known for its *fabada* – a stew of white beans and pork sausage. In Navarra, away from the sea, trout and game play a bigger part.

Whatever the glories of Basque or Spanish cooking at its best, meals in hotels are unlikely to reveal them to you; hotel cooking is in our experience unremarkable – certainly, if good food is a central part of the holiday for you it's important to plan your trip with care so as to dine out in restaurants whenever possible, choosing them with the aid of the Michelin Red Guide. Hotel food is not actually bad – it's just that it's unexciting, with the emphasis more on substantial quantities of plain ingredients than on imagination or subtlety. There is usually a fair range of meat and fish dishes, and occasionally main-course dishes based on eggs or vegetables – for vegetarians, a holiday here wouldn't be quite such hard work as in France. Most tourist hotels make an attempt to provide an English translation of the menu.

Hotel breakfasts are superficially splendid – especially in Paradores, which lay on an impressive buffet spread varying very little from hotel to hotel – but rarely come up to expectations: the fruit is usually canned, the juice unrecognisable, the bread and cakes left over from the day before. Sometimes there are hot dishes – eggs, bacon, sausages – but you have to get in there early. If you like doughnuts for breakfast, *churros* (finger-shaped fritters) are not a bad substitute.

Meal times take some getting used to. Breakfast usually starts at a reasonable hour – 8am or 8.30am – but goes on until about 11am. Lunch doesn't start until 1pm, and most Spanish people have it later than that; it goes on until 3.30pm or 4pm. Dinner in hotels normally starts at 9pm – the hour is greeted by a stampede of starving British and American tourists into the dining room – but occasionally starts even later.

A full three-course meal is a substantial affair in this area, and it will be an energetic or gluttonous tourist who could regularly cope with two a day. You don't have to eat full meals when you sit down to lunch or dinner – in hotels and restaurants you can order individual dishes; but a particularly satisfying way to fill in between major bouts is to have some *tapas*.

Tapas are small dishes of food which you can have either singly or in combination, served in most bars (including many hotel bars) at the times when you might otherwise have a proper meal. The word *tapa* means 'lid', and one convincing explanation of how it came to be used in this way goes back to the days when horsemen would expect to be able to refresh themselves at an inn without dismounting. The innkeeper would hand up a jug of wine and, if the traveller was someone important, would often balance some titbit on the cloth or parchment covering the jug as a gesture of hospitality – rather in the way that you sometimes find a bowl of peanuts on a modern bar; over the years, the special treat for VIPs became the normal practice, expected by everyone – and *tapas* were still served free along with drinks until the time of the Civil War. They're no longer free, but still a good-value and interesting way of having a snack.

Anything and everything is liable to be served as *tapas* – cheese, vegetables, cooked meats, seafood, *chorizos* (spicy red sausage), omelettes – normally the thick, filling *tortilla española*, built around potatoes and onions.

Wine

For wine lovers, one of the attractions of a holiday in Northern Spain is bound to be the prospect of getting on first-name terms with the wines of Rioja. The province of La Rioja lies to the south of the coastal mountains at the eastern end of the area covered by this book, with its vineyards straddling the Rio Ebro. It's not an area which goes out of its way to encourage vineyard tours and tastings in the way that many French wine-producing areas do, though it is possible to visit several *bodegas* nonetheless – see the 'base' entry for Santo Domingo de la Calzada, on page 121. For most people, the wine-lists of the hotels you're staying in will offer quite enough of an opportunity to explore La Rioja without even going there.

The wines for which La Rioja is famous are *tintos*, reds – full-bodied, fruity wines with a distinctive 'vanilla' flavour that comes from the time spent maturing in oak barrels. The ageing period of the wine – both in the barrel and in the bottle – can vary widely; the best, 'biggest' wines of a given vintage will be selected to become *Gran Reservas*, and aged for at least two years in the barrel and a further three in the bottle before being put on sale; less grand wines will be aged for at least three years, of which at least one must be spent in the barrel, and then sold as *Reservas*; and ordinary wines will be aged for one year each in barrel and bottle, before being sold as *Crianza* or *Con Crianza* – literally, 'with nursery'. Wine which has had no barrel ageing at all may have no categorising label (there's often a separate label on the back of the bottle, if the main one doesn't give this information) or it may be labelled *Sin Crianza* – 'without nursery'.

There are white Riojas, and very good they can be too – provided you get them in the right condition. Traditionally, white Rioja has been at its best after several years maturing in the cask to allow its sharp taste to mellow; some *bodegas* are still making their wines this way, but most white Rioja is now made to be drunk young – one or two years old. The rule is to drink the youngest vintage available unless the wine is labelled as a *Crianza* or a *Reserva*, meaning that it has been deliberately aged before bottling (usually for a shorter time than the red wines).

The *bodegas* (literally 'cellars') are wine-making establishments which often use grapes from a wide area, and bear more resemblance to a brewery than they do to the quaint wine properties of France – and it's the names of the *bodegas* (or their owners) which identify the wines, rather than any information about the localities in which they originate or the grapes from which they're made, or who grew them. The wines of La Rioja are now quite common in Britain – much more so than a few years ago, when they were something of a secret bargain. If you take an interest in good-value, mid-priced wines at home, many of the names you'll meet in Spain will be familiar: Paternina, La Rioja Alta, Berberana, Campo Viejo, Marqués de Murrieta, Marqués de Riscal, Marqués de Cáceres, CUNE, for example. The Parador chain of hotels has its own brand of Rioja, which is actually made by Marqués de Cáceres and is extremely good value. Most of the finer Riojas are made in the area west of Logroño – in Rioja Alta, south of the Río Ebro, and Rioja Alavesa, north of the river; Rioja Baja, east of Logroño, makes relatively strong, coarse wines.

Not surprisingly, prices throughout Northern Spain are a lot lower than you'll be used to paying in Britain – very satisfactory Rioja can be had for as little as £2 a bottle in restaurants, well under £1 a bottle in supermarkets. Very grand wines typically cost around £6 in restaurants, and there's a whole range of alternatives in between. You'll have plenty of opportunity to make up your own mind about what gives best value, but a good starting point among the reds is a *Reserva* or *Gran Reserva* that's about six to ten years old. Be wary of much older, much more expensive wines: they need to have been very classy indeed in the first place to be good value after twenty years, and the further you go back into the murky history of Rioja-making, the more it's likely that you'll meet wines of very mixed parentage. The best recent red vintages have been 1975, 1976, 1978 and 1981.

Rioja isn't the only wine sold or made in Northern Spain, even if it is the only one you're likely to have come across at home. The adjoining province of Navarra, to the north-east, is up and coming, with a range of good reds and whites – some of which stand comparison with Riojas. As in Rioja, there are aged wines sold as *Reservas*, which you can expect to be quite a bit cheaper than the product from across the county line; and there are spicy younger wines that are cheaper still. The less sun-blessed regions near the north and west coasts produce *vino verde* – slightly sparkling, sharp-tasting 'green wines', much like the better-known Portuguese version; Albariño del Palacio from near Cambados is a good example. Much stronger, still whites are produced in the Monterrey/Verín area.

ON THE ROAD

What's involved in getting around

To get the most out of your visit to Northern Spain, a car is essential. It is possible to travel through the region by train or bus – indeed the rail journey from Santander to Oviedo, which closely follows that marvellously wild stretch of coast, has many British enthusiasts who are delighted to take this five-hour rail journey again and again. But for most practical purposes getting by without a car would be extremely difficult – as we shall see later, even with a car it can sometimes be difficult enough.

Advance preparations

If you're taking your car with you, you will need the following:

* A Green Card from your insurance company (Spanish customs at Santander will ask you to produce it)
* Your car registration document
* A Bail Bond (this can be obtained from your insurance company; if you take the AA Five Star insurance package, a Bail Bond will be included at no extra cost)
* A spare set of bulbs and a red warning triangle
* Breakdown insurance: you might consider it useful to take out a motoring insurance policy offered by the AA or Europ Assistance which provides 24-hr emergency help if you break down or have an accident. The cost for 14-day cover, together with medical and personal goods cover, works out at around £50 for a couple and their car.

Making plans

When you plan your itinerary, be extremely conservative in the number of miles you plan to cover. Places may look reasonably close together on the map, but don't be deceived. In many places, particularly in mountain areas and on a number of the coast roads, driving can be very slow going. This is partly because the roads themselves are not terribly good – in some provinces there are more pot-holes than road; partly because they twist and turn; but mostly because the main roads tend to be choked with lorries. Almost all goods in Northern Spain appear to be shifted by road – so it's common on slow mountain roads to see huge tailbacks of traffic proceeding behind a chain of lorries. And not only is the driving slow – it can also be exhausting. So don't attempt to do too much; 100 miles in a day would be a sensible maximum – unless of course, you have the advantage of using a stretch of motorway or an improved three-lane road. The roads south of the Cantabrian Cordillera, east and west from León, cross flatter country and tend to offer faster, more relaxing driving.

Roads are divided into inter-provincial 'N' roads and local 'C' roads. While 'N' roads are usually *better* than 'C' roads, don't assume that they're actually *good*. In the mountain areas, 'N' roads are likely to prove fairly basic. Most mountain residents drive around in the locally manufactured version of the Land Rover – and you will soon discover why. All mountain roads must be driven very slowly. On many bends, a complete absence of any banking means that 30mph could prove a dangerously high speed.

There is a plan to construct a motorway which will link the whole of Northern Spain; rather like the Channel Tunnel, you should believe it when you see it. At the moment, there is motorway only from the French border to Bilbao, where it heads south-west to Burgos, or south-east to Logroño and Zaragoza. There is also motorway from Pamplona to Zaragoza.

Moving westwards, motorways become a rarity. There is a particularly valuable stretch from just south of Oviedo which takes you over the mountains to León. If you're travelling west from Santander to Galicia, we would suggest using this motorway and going west from León in order to avoid using the dreadful N634 (see 'The world's worst road', below). There are short stretches of motorway linking Gijón and Avilés both with each other and Oviedo. Don't be tempted to take the coast road from Ribadesella to Luarca via Gijón and Avilés because of its attractive-looking short stretch of motorway. The drive, apart from the motorway, takes you along an exceptionally beautiful stretch of coast; but it is mind-numbingly slow.

There are two other short pieces of motorway in the north: one links Santiago and La Coruña, the other goes from Vigo to Pontevedra. Both are well worth using.

There are charges for using motorways in Spain; but they are so small, you wonder whether it's worth anybody's while collecting them.

The world's worst road

'The roads in the Asturias, much like those of Galicia, savour more of the age of Adam than of Macadam,' wrote Richard Ford in 1855. Things have changed very little in the Asturias and parts of Galicia, and a few other places, where the roads are in an execrable state. If there were ever a competition for the world's worst road, the N634 coast road from Ribadeo to Bilbao would probably start as favourite. With the exception of an improved stretch from Ribadesella to Torrelavega, the N634 is absolutely appalling.

From Ribadeo to Luarca, the road is reasonably straight; but an improvement scheme is in progress along almost the whole length. In some countries, they would complete one three-mile stretch before moving on to next. Not in Northern Spain; instead, they've started work on the entire 40-mile stretch all in one go; they've built a bridge here and a by-pass there, but nothing actually joins up. There are stretches of two or three miles where there is no tarmac at all. Nobody is hazarding a guess at when the improvements will be completed; this year, next year, sometime, never ... check with the Brittany Ferries office in Santander to discover the latest state of play.

From Luarca to Oviedo, the road switchbacks up the mountains with some dreadful twists and turns and a number of appalling sheer drops. From Oviedo to Santander, the road improves and becomes excellent from Ribadesella. From Santander to Bilbao, however, the N634 degenerates badly. This 60-mile stretch twists and turns along the coast, with inevitable convoys stuck behind lorries belching clouds of exhaust fumes.

Reminders

Overtaking One of the first things you have to learn is how to overtake lorries safely. Fortunately, Spanish lorry drivers (unlike their British counterparts) aren't fired with a desire to see all car users turned to jam. When you get behind a lorry, the driver will indicate to you whether it is safe for you to overtake; if it is not safe, he will turn on his left indicator, if it is safe he will flash his right-hand indicator. Don't take his opinion as gospel – more a rough guide to whether overtaking is at all possible. Give him a toot as you go by to let him know you are overtaking.

Traffic police Spanish motorcycle cops look a pretty determined bunch. They always work in pairs, and like nothing better than to hand out an on-the-spot fine for speeding or overtaking in a forbidden spot (approaching the brow of a hill or where the road signs say overtaking is not allowed). As in Britain, Spanish road users are keen to warn other drivers of the presence of the police – they'll flash their headlights to announce that a speed trap is in progress around the next bend.

Petrol No garages accept credit cards, so make sure you always have enough cash to pay for petrol. Petrol is slightly cheaper in Spain than in Britain. In rural and mountain areas, petrol stations can be few and very far between; always fill up when you have the chance – and take a spare can with you in case of emergencies.

Security Never leave valuables in an unattended car; in towns, if you're staying overnight, always park your car off the street if you can.

The West

Bagpipers, warm hospitality, an attractive climate, a beautiful coastline with its distinctive *rías*; and at the heart of Galicia, the magnificent city of Santiago de Compostela, journey's end for million upon million of pilgrims.

■ BASES IN THE WEST

We have divided Northern Spain into three: the West, the Centre and the East. In each area we have sifted out those villages, towns or cities which you will probably want to use as a base – because there are interesting sights or good hotels to be found there.

Each base is the subject of a separate short chapter which provides a brief account of the place as a whole, followed by details of the sights you should see, the attractions that can be found in places nearby, the hotel or hotels where you should stay – and alternative accommodation you might consider if rooms don't happen to be available in our selected hotels. We have also included, where appropriate, comments from holidaymakers who have completed questionnaires distributed by Brittany Ferries and from readers who have taken the first edition of the guide with them on holiday in Northern Spain.

These are our bases in the West:

Hotel prices are indicated by ratings. In 1987, prices for a double room with bath are roughly as follows:

£	under £20
££	£20 to £30
£££	£30 to £40
££££	£40 to £55
£££££	£55 to £75

INTRODUCTION

This is Galicia: Celtic Spain – where even the coastline somehow contrives to resemble the craggy Celtic coastlines of Brittany, Ireland, Wales, Cornwall and Scotland. There is a passion for the bagpipes, and a Celtic fondness for fiestas of singing, dancing and making merry. And, as in most Celtic countries, when it rains it comes down like stair-rods.

This is the favourite region of many people who know Spain well. There is much to see: there are more than 35,000 villages and towns to be found among its mountains and valleys; there are a thousand rivers – and a thousand beaches, coves and inlets along the length of its 3,000km coastline.

From the gentle, wooded coastline of the Rías Bajas around Bayona and Vigo to the jagged mountains around Verín and Orense, it is a land of changing scenery and frequent surprises. Perhaps the biggest surprise is Santiago de Compostela. Protestant Britain has now forgotten the significance of this city which during the Middle Ages ranked with Rome and Jerusalem as a place of pilgrimage. The legend of St James, whose body is said to rest here, may be no more than a legend; the city itself, and its beautiful squares and buildings, is certainly real enough.

This is an area for gentle exploration. The roads are good enough, the food is tasty and there are superb hotels. The Parador at Bayona is reckoned by many to be the best in Spain, but all the Paradores here in Galicia are fine enough. The problem is deciding which places you can afford to leave out of your itinerary.

If you make it as far as Bayona, you will want to include a short trip from Túy across the Portuguese border to Valença do Minho and stay a night or two at its splendid Pousada within the ancient walled city. Northern Portugal has many other attractions which could detain you, particularly its *casas antigas* – manor houses which offer luxurious bed-and-breakfast accommodation. You must also take in Verín with its own fine Parador, standing beside the nearest thing to an enchanted castle that you're likely to see. Pontevedra, with its fascinating museum and its maze of old streets, is also a must. And you shouldn't neglect to visit La Coruña nor the old city of Lugo with its solid slate walls.

That's just for starters; perhaps it's time to think about extending your holiday...!

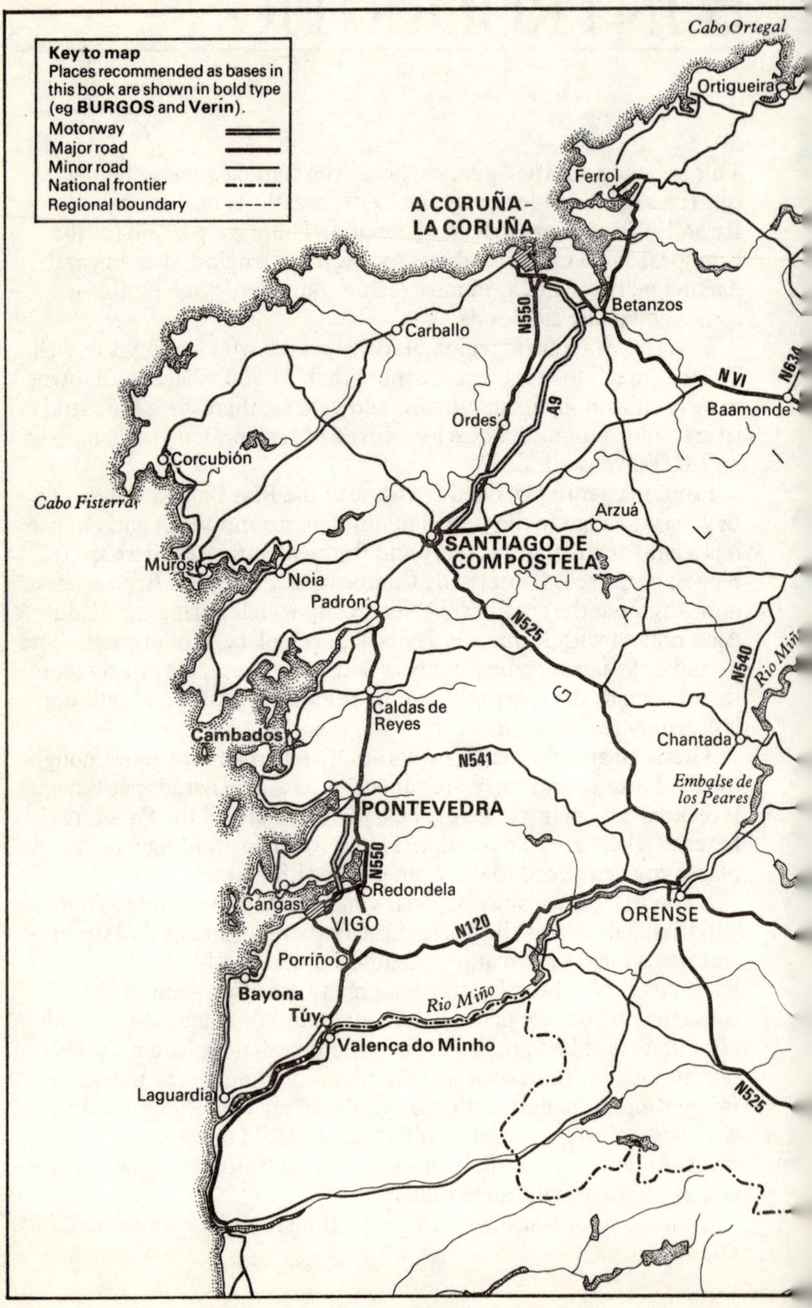
Key to map
Places recommended as bases in this book are shown in bold type (eg **BURGOS** and **Verin**).
Motorway
Major road
Minor road
National frontier
Regional boundary
Cabo Ortegal
Ortigueira
Ferrol
A CORUÑA - LA CORUÑA
Betanzos
N550
Carballo
N VI
N634
Baamonde
A9
Ordes
Corcubión
Cabo Fisterra
Arzuá
SANTIAGO DE COMPOSTELA
Muros
Noia
Padrón
N525
G
A
L
I
N540
Río Miño
Caldas de Reyes
Cambados
Chantada
N541
Embalse de los Peares
PONTEVEDRA
N550
Redondela
Cangas
VIGO
N120
ORENSE
Porriño
Bayona
Río Miño
Túy
Valença do Minho
Laguardia
N525

Costa Verde
Foz
Ribadeo
N634
Castropol
Mondoñedo
Vegadeo
Luarca
Avilés
llalba
LUGO
Rio Navia
Puerto de Palo
Tineo
N630
N VI
Puerto de Pedrafita do Cebreiro
Villafranca del Bierzo
nfort
Lemos
o Sil
N120
A Gudiña
erín
Puebla de Sanabria
PORTUGAL
N VI
N630

■ BAYONA

When British travellers meet up in a Parador bar for a pre-dinner sherry or two at the end of a hard dusty day on the road, there tends to be only one serious topic of conversation. Which Parador did you stay in last, what was it like, where are you planning to stay next – and does anybody know how good it is? Are there mini-bars, how grand is the breakfast, is there perhaps a swimming pool? This intelligence is traded as carefully as Inca gold. Today's pilgrims on the roads of Northern Spain are not searching for the spiritual goal of Santiago de Compostela, they are on a rather more sensual quest: they travel in the hope of finding the Perfect Parador.

So, after a few more sherries and a few plates of *tapas*, the conversation begins to get more philosophical and people start to reflect on the Big Question: which is the Best Ever Parador? The real *aficionados* smile knowingly; but even those who have never been there and those, conscious of the cruel vicissitudes of life, who fear they never will, have the answer to this one: Bayona.

Bayona, they whisper reverentially (say it soft, and it's almost like praying...). Its reputation runs before it throughout the Parador circuit – it stands there at the bottom left-hand corner of Galicia, almost at the furthest point west of Northern Spain, as the Ultimate Goal, the Big Apple. Have you been to Bayona, you will be asked; you'd do well not to be found wanting in the reply.

Not only does Bayona have a great Parador, it is also a superb seaside town, at the mouth of the Vigo *ría*, with marvellous views across to the Cies islands. Bayona also has a notable place in history as the first place in the Old World to learn of the discovery of the New World: it was here that the Pinta arrived in 1493 with the news of Columbus's discovery. (In Bayona lies buried the first Indian brought back to the Old World on the Pinta.)

▶ What to see

Monte Real 'What to see' and 'Where to stay' amount to the same thing, because the Bayona Parador is situated within the Monte Real, a huge 16th-century fort covering an 18-hectare area on the headland circled by two miles of battlements. Standing on the headland, the sea appears to surround you completely; on one side a stylish yachting club nestling alongside a fishing harbour, on others the Bayona and Vigo *rías* and the lush green hills beyond.

▶ Nearby

The coast The coastal strip north and south of Bayona is just about the most seductively beautiful area of Northern Spain, comparable to the best of the French Riviera – or at least how the Riviera must have looked before it was despoiled by tourism.

The drive over to Bayona from Túy takes you through gently rolling hills and sweet-smelling pine and eucalyptus forests. At the highest point of the road, you suddenly glimpse the view on the other side of the hills: the Rías Bajas, and particularly the exquisite Vigo Ría – a sheet of glistening blue water, lapping against alabaster-white beaches. And everything so quiet and peaceful – the serenity intensified by the sheer beauty of the scene spread out before you.

Vigo NE, 20km by road. Major ports are normally places to steer well clear of when you're on holiday; it's difficult to think of any major British or French port, for example, where you would happily choose to spend a day. Vigo is certainly a major port (it is Spain's largest fishing port) but it is not at all disagreeable. It is a neat place with carefully tended flower gardens and clean streets. It boasts one of the best climates in Northern Spain – and enjoys an outstandingly beautiful setting beside the wide *ría* and framed by the ubiquitous wooded slopes. Vigo no longer receives the regular calls of the big liners at its imposing transatlantic terminal, which now stands looking rather forlorn and miserable beside the harbour. But it is

Yacht marina at Bayona

still busy and thriving – and for those who have had a surfeit of Romanesque churches and carved altar-pieces, it will probably come as a welcome change to 'do' Vigo's shops and department stores (particularly El Corte Inglés). Vigo also has an old town and fishermen's quarter with bars and restaurants, and what looked suspiciously like a red-light district (which certainly does make a change from Plateresque exteriors).

▶ Where to stay

Parador Nacional Conde de Gondomar ££££ ☎ 986 355000
Although Bayona can fairly claim the finest and most beautifully located Parador in Northern Spain, set on its own promontory with most rooms overlooking the sea, it isn't perfect: we have to record a number of critical reports from readers who stayed there during 1986. Perhaps the Parador is a victim of its own success: several readers reported indifferent service and an impersonal staff. There were also moans about day-trippers, particularly on weekends and holidays, who flood the promontory – and who seem to wander at will around the gardens and pool, ogling swimmers and sunbathers. We re-visited Bayona in August 1986, and were unhappily forced to find the hotel guilty as charged. And yet it remains one of our favourites; as one reader conceded, you can forgive a few shortcomings in a hotel which enjoys such a splendid site.

The building itself is in the style of a typical Galician *pazo* or manor house. Facilities include a nearby beach, a swimming pool, a tennis court and a sauna. The public rooms are as palatial as you would expect in such a historic monument. The bedrooms are elegantly and comfortably furnished – but their most prized asset is the spectacular view that most offer of the sea.

Holidaymakers' reports

'Our favourite hotel: the location, accommodation and food were all superb; service at reception is poor' Mr & Mrs J N Barnikel

'Our favourite hotel: excellent' Mr & Mrs E Wood

'Food was good but hotel was impersonal' Roger & Nicola Mortimer

'Quite frankly we were disappointed' Dr P Blackwell-Smyth

Alternatives Vigo has a couple of good hotels. The four-star Ciudad de Vigo (£££ ☎ 986 227820) is a smart businessman's hotel in an attractive part of the city. The four-star Bahia de Vigo (£££ ☎ 986 226700) stands opposite the old transatlantic terminal, and has a jolly, nautical style: the staff dress like naval officers; public areas like the bar are fitted out like ships with port-holes and diving helmets aplenty.

LA CORUÑA

You can choose from three pronunciations: in Galician it's A Coruña, the Castilian way is La Coruña, while we British call it Corunna. It's perhaps the only city in Northern Spain that many British people have ever heard of, because it has played a couple of walk-on parts in English history. It was from here on 22 July 1588 that Philip II's Armada of 130 men o' war launched its ill-fated attack on England. Almost 15,000 lives and half the Armada's ships were lost in the disastrous defeat which followed, marking the turning point of Spain's fortunes as a world power. A year later, in an attempt to capitalise on Britain's advantage, Drake sailed into La Coruña with 30 ships and 15,000 men as part of a plan to gain the crown for Portuguese pretender Dom Antonio. According to legend, the plan was foiled by Maria Pita, who plucked the English standard from the beacon and raised the alarm.

But perhaps the reason why La Coruña is lodged so firmly in the British consciousness is because of Sir John Moore, who was killed in the Battle of Elvina during the Napoleonic wars. The poem written about the event by Charles Wolfe has been reluctantly committed to memory by million upon million of British school-children (some of this dread poem is printed below, but see if you can recall a few lines before stealing a look).

La Coruña's problem is that one expects too much of it. You know its name, you know it has a famous place in history – so you expect great sights. Certainly there are some things worth seeing, but nothing sensational. The glazed balconies are a fine spectacle, the streets in the old town are pleasant – but there is nothing to compare with Santiago or Pontevedra. If you come here not expecting too much but simply to enjoy its easy-going charm, you won't be disappointed.

Don't be tempted to venture out in La Coruña without a raincoat and/or an umbrella; along with nearby Santiago, residents reckon that this is the rainfall capital of the world. The locals say that if you can't see across the estuary to Ferrol, then it's raining – and if you can see across the estuary, then rain must be on the way!

Holidaymakers' reports

'The main thing which impressed me about La Coruña is the marked difference in the way of life between the city and the countryside five to ten kilometres outside it' Derek Greenhalgh

▶ What to see

The Tomb of Sir John Moore The former San Carlos fort where Sir John Moore is buried is now a public garden, a few minutes' walk from the Hotel Finisterre. Next to a look-out point which offers a sweeping view across the large harbour, you can study Charles Wolfe's famous poem:

The Burial of Sir John Moore
(fragment)

Not a drum was heard, not a funeral note,
As his corse to the rampart we hurried;
Not a soldier discharged his farewell shot
O'er the grave where our hero we buried

We buried him darkly at dead of night,
The sods with our bayonets turning,
By the struggling moonbeam's misty light
And the lantern dimly burning.

No useless coffin enclosed his breast,
Not in sheet or in shroud we wound him;
But he lay like a warrior taking his rest,
With his martial cloak around him.

Few and short were the prayers we said,
And we spoke not a word of sorrow;
But we steadfastly gazed on the face that was dead,
And we bitterly thought of the morrow.

Slowly and sadly we laid him down,
From the field of his fame fresh and gory;
We carved not a line, and we raised not a stone –
But we left him alone with his glory.

Hercules Tower Built on a northern headland by the Romans in the 2nd century, the tower was rebuilt into its present shape in 1790. It is reckoned to be the oldest working lighthouse in the world.

Glazed balconies Glazed balconies are a feature of Northern Spain, especially Galicia, but particularly La Coruña. The tall houses on Avenida de la Marina are famous for their balconies, and look very striking – even more so with the sun flashing from the glass at sunset.

▶ Nearby

Ferrol NE, 60km by road. We have a sneaking suspicion that the only reason that Ferrol has a Parador is that this town is the birthplace of Franco – it's not difficult to imagine some sycophantic government bureaucrat awarding the town a Parador in the hope of currying favour with the Generalissimo. Ferrol is one of Spain's most important naval bases; it has some interesting old streets (but then again, what Spanish town or city has not?) and a one-way traffic system that makes Hampton Court maze seem like child's play. The Parador (££ ☎ 981 356720) is satisfactory but very poorly located, and not so good as to be a goal in itself.

▶ Where to stay

Hotel Finisterre £££ ☎ 981 205400 This four-star hotel, part of the HUSA group, is agreeably located on the sea-front and is first choice in most respects – particularly for its sports complex, with three swimming pools and tennis courts. Regrettably, service is generally indifferent, and occasionally worse – we arrived to take lunch at 3.15pm (the restaurant was said to be open until 3.45pm) and were treated to much sighing and gnashing of teeth by the restaurant staff, who then proceeded to set an all-comers' record for Spain by serving a complete lunch in half an hour flat. The rooms are slightly cramped but comfortably furnished – ask for one that offers a spectacular view over the busy harbour, which seems to be at work 24 hours a day, unloading cargo vessels or repairing fishing boats.

Alternatives The four-star Hotel Atlantico (£££ ☎ 981 226500) doesn't have the advantage of the Finisterre's swimming pools or its location slap bang next to the sea, but it is newer and the service seems slicker and more efficient – and it has an attractive setting in gardens close to the sea-front. Also highly rated by reporters is the Ciudad de la Coruña (££ ☎ 981 211100), formerly the Eurotel: 'This is a first-class hotel; not expensive and very, very clean. The food and service at its restaurant is excellent, and it also has a swimming pool. This is the best hotel I have stayed at in La Coruña – from the first moment you enter the hotel the staff do everything possible to help make your stay pleasant. It is in my opinion much better than the more expensive hotels such as the Finisterre and Atlantico' Derek Greenhalgh; 'Service and food very good' Dr P Blackwell-Smyth.

■ PONTEVEDRA

The outskirts of Pontevedra are distinctly unpromising but, as with so many other towns in Northern Spain, while the new parts of the city sprawl outwards without much apparent planning or design, the old town at the centre remains almost entirely unchanged.

Pontevedra was once a busy port on the Lerez delta, a centre for fishermen, merchants and traders; but by the 18th century the delta had silted up, forcing sea traffic to use the port at nearby Marin. The city seems not to have suffered unduly from this set-back; today it is a bustling place, with a prosperous population and dozens of well-stocked shops.

Its main attraction, however, is the fascinating old town, lying in a compact area around the Parador, near the Puente del Burgo. Narrow streets run up the hill, mostly undisturbed by traffic – the air is full of the song of birds kept in cages high up on the balconies of ancient pillared houses, each house with its own coat of arms. There are several squares, many with their own Calvary Cross. At the top of the hill lie the public gardens; in the evenings and on Sunday afternoons – as in so many Spanish towns – they are full of smartly dressed families out to take the air, to meet friends or simply to watch the world go by.

► What to see

Cathedral Built by the mariners' guild in the 15th and 16th centuries, this church has an impressive Plateresque west front – the carving is dominated by the crucifixion surrounded by fishermen pulling in their nets.

Provincial museum The museum, situated in two very fine 18th-century houses, is perhaps the best of its sort in the whole of Northern Spain. The most unusual exhibit is the cabin of Admiral Mendez Nunez and the officers' mess of the ship 'Numancia', reached down a dimly lit hatchway. The Admiral earned his place in Spanish history during the Battle of Callao against Peru, when he was accused of reckless judgement for attempting to attack such a stoutly defended port. 'Spain prefers honour without ships to ships without honour,' he said. Other things on show include prehistoric and pre-Roman finds, particularly the spectacular Celtic Golada treasure. Exhibits also provide glimpses of Galician life in former times – including the reconstruction of a typical Galician kitchen. Best of all is an exhibition of fine paintings by local artist Castelao.

▶ Nearby

Cambados NW, 25km by road. Cambados has an attractive setting beside the sea, but unfortunately no beach. The town is pleasant enough: there is an especially good square at the northern entrance, the Plaza de Fefinanes, with a fine *pazo* (Galician manor house) and a 17th-century church, but there is little to persuade the visitor to stay here for some time – except perhaps the Parador. The Parador Nacional del Albarino (£££ ☎ 986 542250) is stylishly built around an old house with large gardens, attractively furnished rooms and a friendly, welcoming staff.

In old Pontevedra

Rías Bajas Pontevedra lies at the heart of the outstandingly attractive Rías Bajas. A *ría* is a sunken river valley like the Scottish firths or the fjords of Norway, and the four particular inlets known as the Rías Bajas run from Muros in the north down to Bayona in the south. Throughout their length, they offer gentle coastal scenery: wooded hills and beautiful beaches interspersed with quiet, contented fishing villages. Places worth visiting include the Mirador de la Curota, west of Padrón, which at a height of 500 metres gives marvellous views (on a clear day) over the four inlets of the Rías Bajas and north to Spain's Land's End, Cabo Fisterra. Sangenjo is perhaps the best of the seaside places; it boasts one of the best climates in the province. The island of La Toja is also very pleasant – but work is in progress on a new tourist development which looks as if it might restrict entry to the general public. The loveliest of all the Rías Bajas in our opinion is the Vigo Ría, which has the fine resort of Bayona at its lower end.

Vigo SW, 25km by road. See Bayona.

▶ Where to stay

Parador Nacional Casa del Barón £££ ☎ 986 855800 Truly accommodation fit for a Baron. From the outside, the Parador looks as if it has been squeezed into a tiny, inadequate residence in Pontevedra's beguiling old town. But it's rather like Doctor Who's Tardis – step inside the hotel, and there is a tremendous sense of spaciousness, particularly on the upper floors. Somehow the designers have managed to contrive a huge garden up on the second floor, with a wide sun-trap lawn, tables and chairs – and even a fir tree (one wonders where the roots go to!). In other parts of the hotel, there are patio courtyards – and outside the restaurant and TV lounge, another attractive garden complete with a fountain.
Holidaymakers' reports
'All the good points of the Paradores: a friendly, efficient, clean manor-house atmosphere – with good food' D R Millar
'Very friendly and welcoming' Mrs A Vile

Alternatives The three-star Hotel Rías Bajas (££ ☎ 986 855100) may not be able to match the Parador in style or ambience, but it is nevertheless a very welcoming establishment, with cosy wood-panelled public rooms offering comfy leather armchairs.

RIBADEO

For those who make the tortuous and extremely bumpy drive west from Oviedo and Luarca, Ribadeo seems forever in the distance, like the Celestial City. As you twist and turn round the endless bends, almost certainly engulfed in the exhaust of a milk tanker, the signposts for Ribadeo become an insistent reminder of your slow progress. Then, as you round a bend in Castropol, Ribadeo suddenly stands before you, shimmering across the estuary like a mirage. Surely, it's now only a few minutes away – but no, the road has one final twist in store, as it takes you 9km to the head of the *ría* and the town of Vegadeo before finally swinging back for the last 10km to Ribadeo. (A road bridge is being built across the estuary as part of the general road improvement from Luarca to Ribadeo, which should eventually make this final twist unnecessary.)

Practically the first building to greet you on your right as you enter the town is the Parador: an ordinary-looking building, in what seems an ordinary location – but the Parador is in fact comfortably furnished within, and the bedrooms offer magnificent views across the estuary to Castropol, a delightful village topped by a church with an inverted-golf-tee spire. Ten minutes on the balcony of your room – sipping a stiff drink from the mini-bar, listening to the church bell tolling soulfully across the water and contemplating the estuary and the activities of the busy little fishing harbour below the Parador – should be enough to remove the tiredness of the road and sharpen the appetite for dinner.

Most people are happy enough to use Ribadeo and its Parador as an overnight staging post before beginning the much less arduous drive on to Lugo or La Coruña. But the town and the surrounding countryside and coastline have plenty more to offer for those prepared to investigate. Ribadeo has nothing that could be classified as a tourist attraction. But it has a busy market selling fish brought in that morning to the harbour, and a wide variety of fresh fruit and vegetables from all parts of Spain. It has a pleasant square with some delightful Art Nouveau buildings, relics of the time when Ribadeo was an important trading port. But rather than having things to see, Ribadeo is essentially a place to enjoy for its easy going charm and soft Galician temperament.

Travelling west out of Ribadeo on the road towards Ferrol and La Coruña, there is a succession of pleasant, clean sandy beaches that you may well find deserted. The first one, Playa de Dos Castros, is nearly five miles from Ribadeo and offers an extremely agreeable spot to spend a few hours: relaxing with a picnic that must include some Galician cheese and a bottle of the superb local Pazo Ribeiro white wine.

▶ Nearby

Mondoñedo SW, 35km by road. We were fortunate to pass through the charming little town of Mondoñedo on the day of its autumn San Lucas fiesta. People from local villages were pouring in to enjoy the marvellous carnival atmosphere. There were Galician pipers striding through the town, filling the streets with the curious, chanting sound of their music.

There were school-children dressed in local costume preparing to compete in the dancing competition. There were stunningly attractive dark-eyed girls ready to take part in the fiesta's beauty contest. And there were men on stilts dressed in the costumes of giant kings and queens, and other performers concealed in the giant heads of Popeye, the Devil and a hideous witch. The market was thronged with dozens of local women selling their small amounts of produce: mouth-watering onions, sweet chestnuts, cooking apples. The men were taking in a drink in the bars, weighing up the merits of the latest garden sieves or getting their scythe sharpened by the mobile knife-grinder. There were jet-black North Africans selling leather handbags and there were gypsy ladies with bloated stomachs begging in the streets.

Even without the excitement of the fiesta, Mondoñedo is a pleasure to visit: it is a beautiful town in an equally beautiful setting. The streets of the old town which run down towards the cathedral are made up of smart white houses with slate roofs – many boasting their own escutcheons. The sunset-coloured stone cathedral, with its Baroque façade, stands imposingly in a marvellous little square of arcaded houses. Inside the cathedral you will find some fascinating 14th-century frescoes, one illustrating the Massacre of the Innocents. There is also a wooden statue of the Virgin, known as the English Virgin, which is believed to have been smuggled away from St Paul's cathedral at the time of the Reformation.

Rías Altas Where the Rías Bajas on the western coast are sheltered and offer a warm climate, the Rías Altas on the northern coast take more of a buffeting from the rough Atlantic and its high winds. The drive along this piece of coastline from Ribadeo to La Coruña is excellent (even if the road itself is not always brilliant). Highlights include the agreeable towns of Foz, with two fine beaches, and Vivero which, at the end of August, holds its Naseiro Romeria – a festival of Galician music and singing.

▶ Where to stay

Parador Nacional de Ribadeo £££ ☎ 982 110825 See the introduction. As far as hotels are concerned, this is really the only game in town. If you can't get a room here, you'll be in a bit of a fix if you're not prepared to accommodate yourself in something less than Parador standard. The nearest alternative Parador is the castle at Villalba, about two hours' drive away – and if Ribadeo is full, you can bet that the six rooms at Villalba will have been reserved weeks ago. So make sure you book a room in Ribadeo well before you set off on your travels.

Holidaymakers' reports

'Lovely locality, good service' Jean Boxall, Doreen Gascoigne

'Our favourite hotel: excellent views' Mrs Matty

■ SANTIAGO DE COMPOSTELA

Santiago de Compostela is Northern Spain's only major tourist attraction. After days of cruising roads and visiting towns practically devoid of holidaymakers, it is rather a surprise to enter a city almost wholly devoted to the business of tourism, with its souvenir shops, beggars and the rest of the baggage that travels in the wake of today's tourist. But tourism is certainly no newcomer to Santiago; in fact, the city can lay claim to being the world's first major tourist destination. At the peak of Santiago's attraction as a place of pilgrimage during the Middle Ages, from the 9th to the 16th century, up to two million people a year (around 5,000 a day) came to worship at what was believed to be the burial place of St James (as a holy place, Santiago was almost the equal of Rome and Jerusalem).

For many pilgrims, Santiago was the end of a long and tiring journey; they came not only from Spain, but from France, Britain, Germany, Italy and Scandinavia. Recognised pilgrimage routes grew up from France through Northern Spain. The pilgrims identified themselves by wearing a uniform of heavy cape, long stave, sandals and a felt hat turned up in front and bearing the scallop-shell emblem of St James. (The scallop shell crops up all over Northern Spain, and its adoption as the emblem of pilgrimage is said to date back to the crusade against the Moorish invaders. The Lord of Pimentel was forced to swim across a *ría*; he miraculously emerged from the sea on the other side covered in scallop shells, which were taken to be the emblem of St James). On their difficult and sometimes dangerous route, the pilgrims were taken care of by Benedictine and Cistercian monks and the Knights Templar of the Spanish Order of the Red Sword, who undertook to guarantee the safety of pilgrims in Northern Spain. Hospitals and hospices were set up to take care of sick and weary pilgrims.

At the end of the 16th century the Reformation in Europe and finally Spain's war with England saw the decline of Santiago as a place of pilgrimage. In 1589 Sir Francis Drake attacked La Coruña, and in a panic the Bishop of Compostela took the cathedral's relics away to a place of safe-keeping. He must have been in too much of a panic, because the relics got lost and remained lost for the next 300 years; they were rediscovered only in 1879, allowing the pilgrimages to start once more. Pilgrimages reach their peak in those years when the feast day of St James, 25 July, falls on a Sunday; that happens next in 1993.

It matters little whether or not you believe in the legend of St James and the value of pilgrimages: Santiago still remains one of Spain's finest cities. Emerging from Calle Franco into Santiago's cathedral square is described by Jan Morris in her incomparable book *Spain* as one of the great moments of travel:

'The square is made of golden granite. In front of you there stands euphonious of name and princely of posture, the Hostal de Los Reyes Católicos, founded by Isabel and Ferdinand as a hostel for pilgrims, and now perhaps the most beautiful hotel in Europe .... Cars seldom cross this celestial plaza, but pedestrians are always about – tourists, hotel pages, policemen, priests; and surveying the calm but never torpid scene, which has a Venetian quality of depth and movement, stands the tall façade of the cathedral, unquestionably one of the great buildings of the world.

'It is like nowehere else. At one end of its enormous block there rises a pyramidical tower of apparently Hindu genesis. In front of its great door two staircases rise so jauntily from the level of the square that they seem to be leading you to some blithe belvedere. And in the centre of the composition the twin west towers of the cathedral soar into the blue in a sensational flourish of Baroque, covered everywhere with balls, bells, stars, crosses, and weathercocks, speckled with green lichens and snapdragons in the crevices, and exuding a delightful air of cheerful satisfaction.'

The legend of St James and Santiago de Compostela The legend has it that the Apostle James the Greater came to Spain to convert the country to Christianity and preached for seven years before returning to Judaea, where he was martyred by Herod. Forced to leave the country, his disciples smuggled St James's body back to Spain and buried it near the spot where they were supposed to have first landed in Spain, near Padrón (a few miles from Santiago). The site of this tomb was unknown for many years but according to legend a star revealed its location to Theodomir, Bishop of Ira Flavia, in 813. ('Compostela' means literally 'field of a star' – from the Latin 'campus stella' – and Santiago is the Spanish for St James.) An alternative legend has it that St James appeared on the battlefield at Clavijo near Logroño, to help the Spaniards in their fight against the Moors; after which time St James became known as 'Matamore' or Slayer of the Moors.

But, as Jan Morris points out: '... in all this, alas, they (the Spanish) are deceiving themselves ... St James, so all the best scholars seem to agree, never came to Spain at all. He was never a soldier. There is no earthly reason why his body should be brought to Galicia, and nothing of the sort is suggested in the Acts of the Apostles, where his death is recorded. He died several centuries before Islam was conceived, probably never mounted a horse in his life, and certainly never slew an infidel .... There is no historical reason why Santiago should be a place of pilgrimage .... It is only an illusion; but so long has it been in the Spanish mind, so attractive is it in itself, that long ago, in the way of all the best hallucinations, it achieved a kind of truth.'

▶ What to see

Cathedral Without a doubt, one of the great buildings of the world; its façade is a Baroque masterpiece, and there are even greater treasures within. The façade stands in front of the original Romanesque exterior, which can be seen as soon as you step inside the doors. Immediately before you is the Door of Glory, an astonishing doorway carved in the 12th century by Master Mateo. At this point, the exhausted pilgrims knew they had reached their journey's end; gratefully they reached out and touched the central pillar, which has become quite worn away from centuries of touching. Master Mateo is also represented on the central pillar beneath St James, and those who pass through the Portico de la Gloria sometimes bump heads with Mateo in the hope of absorbing some of his genius!

The focus of attention within the dark interior of the cathedral is the gleaming 13th-century statue of St James; those pilgrims permitted to climb the stairs behind the altar kiss his richly worked mantle.

The cathedral's museum and treasury are well worth a visit, to see some of the library's valuable religious works and collection of tapestries. In the library you will see a huge incense burner called a *botafumeiro*; on feast days this is hung from the transept dome keystone and, with half a dozen men clinging desperately to the other end of the rope, is swung to the eaves – one year, it is said, the men lost control and the incense burner flew into the square outside.

Plaza de España This magnificent square is bordered on one side by the Baroque façade of the cathedral and the bishop's palace, on the opposite side by the impressive 18th-century town hall, formerly Raxoy Palace. On the square's south side is San Jeronimo College – opposite this, on the north side, is perhaps Santiago's second greatest asset, the Hotel de Los Reyes Católicos, of which more later.

The old streets One of the great pleasures of Santiago is to walk through the old streets that run up to the cathedral. The best are the Rua del Villar, Rua Nueva and Calle Franco; fashionable clothes shops stand next to ancient grocery shops run by wizened old ladies swathed in black. If you're planning to do much walking, remember your umbrella; the rain in Spain seems to stay mainly in Santiago!

Holidaymakers' reports

'Atmosphere of Santiago well suited to walking tour – excellent place for a long weekend with Los Reyes Católicos as your hotel' B E Anderson

The cathedral, with Los Reyes Católicos on the left

▶ Nearby

Cabo Fisterra This is Spain's Land's End; it was once significant not only as the westernmost extremity of Spain – it also represented the western edge of the known world, until Columbus discovered America. Unlike our Land's End, Cabo Fisterra has no souvenir shops or places claiming to be the first and last house in Europe – it is simply a place of wild, unspoilt beauty.

▶ Where to stay

Hotel de Los Reyes Católicos ££££ ☎ 981 582200 Like the Hostal San Marcos in León, this is a five-star grande luxe hotel now run as part of the Parador chain. Again like the San Marcos, Los Reyes Católicos is a hotel set within a building which is both of historic importance and of extraordinary beauty. From the delicately carved Plateresque doorway, through to the four patios built within the Hospital's cross-shaped design, the whole building is an absolute delight.

The Hospital Real de Peregrinos was built in the 16th century on the instructions of the Catholic monarchs Ferdinand and Isabella, to serve as both a pilgrim inn and a hospital. It was converted into a hotel in 1954. It is now a luxury hotel of the very highest quality. The bedrooms are in general lavishly appointed, with canopied beds, richly woven carpets, antique furniture and expensive paintings – though reports from readers make it clear that some of the rooms are distinctly cramped.

Although it is one of the world's finest hotels, and would have to be described as 'posh', the atmosphere of the Los Reyes Católicos is quite different from that of the posh hotels of Britain, where staff can make you feel like dirt if you don't know the 'right' way to behave. Here, the staff do all they can to make you feel welcome – and since the hotel is so spread out around its four patios, you're hardly exposed to the public eye at all. Breakfast is buffet-style, while lunch and dinner are equally relaxed.

It could be argued that the Los Reyes Católicos is an even finer hotel than León's San Marcos, because its location on the Plaza de España, adjacent to the cathedral, would be impossible to better. And if we were pushed to make a choice between the two we would prefer Los Reyes Católicos; but comparing the relative merits of two such great hotels is ultimately pointless – they're 240 miles apart, and you can perfectly well justify including both in your itinerary.

Holidaymakers' reports

'Unquestionably the finest hotel I have ever stayed in' M Quaid

'A magical hotel for a magical city' D Clarkson

'A luxury hotel; bedroom very small' P F MacCabe
'Bedroom was dark and poky' D V May
'Expensive; but what an experience!' Jim Matthews

Alternatives Given the presence of the magnificent Los Reyes Católicos, you might have thought that any other five-star hotel in Santiago would be superfluous. This was indeed the case for many years, but in 1985 a brand new five-star hotel joined the fray. The Hotel Araguaney (££££ ☎ 981 595900) is primarily a business hotel, designed to offer the comforts and conveniences expected by a modern executive. It has a heated swimming pool, solarium and sauna. About 15 minutes' walk from the cathedral, it may be a little too far from the old centre of the town for holidaymakers. Even further from the centre is the four-star Hotel Peregrino (££ ☎ 981 591850) which also has a heated swimming pool and its own discothèque. Unless you're particularly athletic, walking from here to the old centre of the town is impossible. 'Too far from centre, discourteous staff and expensive' P F MacCabe. On the edge of the old town is the four-star Hotel Compostela (££ ☎ 981 585700), which looks a little gloomy but is good value.

■ TÚY

Túy is the principal northern crossing point from Spain to Portugal. It is beautifully situated on a hill overlooking the River Miño and its lush valley. But the town itself, like many other frontier towns, is in parts noisy and rather scruffy; around the Cathedral Square, however, there are some interesting, well preserved old streets which are worth exploring.

But having got so near to Portugal it seems a shame not to go the whole way and see something of it. So, despite the presence of a perfectly acceptable Parador in Túy, our advice is to cross the border to Valença do Minho, which is much more worth visiting than Túy.

▶ What to see

Cathedral If it looks more like a castle than a cathedral, that's because it was formerly a fortress. At the frontier with Portugal, Túy has been in the thick of various historical cross-border battles. Construction of the cathedral citadel began towards the end of the 12th century – and although work on it continued for three centuries, the builders remained faithful to the original Gothic style. The solid columns you can see within are necessary to support the structure of the cathedral against the earthquakes which have been known to strike the area.

▶ Nearby

Valença do Minho Monsieur Eiffel designed the extraordinary double-decker bridge (traffic on one level, trains on another) which crosses the frontier River Minho – which explains why the structure looks suspiciously like a reject section of the Eiffel Tower. Crowds gather at the Portuguese end of the frontier to enjoy the carnival atmosphere which seems to prevail there 24 hours a day (the day we passed through a flock of highly bewildered sheep managed to get involved in the proceedings); don't be surprised if the queues tail back, particularly when returning from Portugal to Spain – waits of an hour or longer at peak times are not uncommon.

The first impression of Portugal is not favourable; the chaotic border post, the terrible road (hundreds of thousands of granite sets cobbled together) and the scruffy state of the new Valença. Don't be put off: your destination is the old town of Valença, situated within a magnificent system of fortifications high above the river.

The town within these walls has been beautifully preserved. In many ways, it looks like a real-life Portmeirion: narrow cobbled streets running between whitewashed houses, large squares flanked by churches and a stage-set town hall. The streets are strikingly bright, with gaily coloured umbrellas outside the many cafés and pastel clothes hanging up outside the tourist shops. Many people seem to come to the old town specifically to buy different sorts of cotton goods, particularly towels and bedspreads.

The Vaubanesque fortress is an extraordinary structure. By the beginning of the 18th century it had become one of the biggest and most important strongholds in Portugal, consisting of double lengths of wall, moats, trenches, covered roads and ramparts. Away from the busy shops and cafés, the town within the fortress exudes an air of immense calm; there are many places on the grassy ramparts where you can relax in the sun and look out over the beautiful valley.

Holidaymakers' reports

'The highlight of our holiday' Mrs K Aldridge

▶ Where to stay

Pousada de São Teotónio ££££ ☎ 051 22252 Pousadas are to Portugal what Paradores are to Spain. The word 'pousada' means literally resting place or inn; like Paradores, Pousadas are normally to be found in quiet, isolated spots by the sea shore, in the mountains or on the plains. Like the Paradores, they are also owned by the state, and are often housed in castles, palaces or historic buildings.

The Valença Pousada enjoys a superb position in a quiet corner of the fortified city, with clear views of the river and across the valley to Túy. The furnishings and décor did not match the best of the Paradores, but the staff were very welcoming – and almost everybody there spoke good English. Try to get a room with a balcony where you can sit out in the evening and absorb the view over a glass of the local *vinho verde*. The food was also enjoyable: particularly good were the salmon caught nearby in the River Minho, and the regional cornmeal bread.

Holidaymakers' reports

'Our favourite hotel' Dr P Blackwell-Smyth

Alternatives For those who have just spent the night at the Verín Parador, the Parador Nacional de Túy (£££ ☎ 986 600309) has a curiously familiar look. It ought to look familiar, because it's exactly the same building – even the standard issue Parador grandfather clock and suit of armour are to be found in the same spots near the stairs that they occupy in Verín. One doesn't object to the Paradores saving money by duplicating their hotel plans – but when each Parador is supposed to have its own special character it does seem to be a bit silly to have built exactly the same hotel a couple of hours down the road. On the other hand, if it looks good in Verín, then you can only say that it looks good here too.

If you cross the border to Valença do Minho and fail to get a room at the Pousada de São Teotónio, and you're feeling extravagant, find out if there are rooms available at the Pousada de Dom Diniz (£££££ ☎ 051 95601), a short drive towards the coast at Vila Nova da Cerveira. This is one of the finest hotels we've seen, set in its own riverside citadel at the heart of an exquisite village.

Further afield If you have time, it is well worth venturing into the magnificent heart of Northern Portugal to see its lush scenery, spectacular valleys, marvellously unspoilt villages – and on the coast, splendid deserted beaches. There is also the chance to stay as a paying guest with the thriving remnants of the Portuguese aristocracy in their stately homes. About an hour's drive from the border is the excellent little town of Ponte de Lima, which lies at the heart of the Alto Minho region. The tourist office here is the booking centre for the 40 manor houses which make up the *Casas Antigas* association; all offer bed and breakfast from around £30 for two people.

The best of the Casas Antigas (literally 'old houses') are the Paços (pronounced 'passos') – houses which were deemed grand enough to accommodate the King should he happen to be in the neighbourhood. The Paço de Calheiros, a few miles above Ponte de Lima, is a magnificent neo-Baroque creation set in a huge estate with spectacular views over the Lima valley. After negotiating the twisting road up to the house, you are likely to be met by the dashing young Count of Calheiros himself. The massive Paço has no fewer than a dozen living rooms, and eight bedrooms for guests – each with private bathroom.

A half-hour's drive from Ponte de Lima on the road to Arcos de Valdavez, above the village of Jolda, is the equally delightful Paço da Gloria, which has been English-owned for over 200 years. The superb location, overlooking the Lima valley, and the ornate swimming pool (only a quarter of the Casas Antigas have a pool) would in themselves be enough to justify a night or two here; but with its luxuriously appointed rooms, the Paço da Gloria is somewhere you could happily linger for a month.

For further information about Casas Antigas, write to: Maria do Ceu Sa Lima, Delegação de Turismo de Ponte do Lima, 4990 Ponte de Lima, Portugal ☎ 942335 Telex: 32618.

■ VERÍN

It would be difficult to imagine a more impressive location for a hotel than the one enjoyed by the Parador Nacional Monterrey on its hill overlooking Verín, the Río Tamaga and the vine-covered slopes that rise up from the wide plain. The Parador takes its name from the magnificent fortress of Monterrey, which stands proudly only a couple of hundred yards along the hill, still in a remarkably well preserved state.

Verín is best known for its Fontenova *agua mineral*, which no doubt will be served to you at some time during your stay. The town itself suffers from being on the main road from Madrid to Orense and Santiago. But away from the heavy through-traffic, the town is delightfully picturesque: there are many houses with glazed balconies overlooking narrow cobbled streets.

▶ What to see

Monterrey Castle W, 6km by road (close to the Parador). Those staying at the Parador will be unable to resist exploring the castle as soon as they have checked in. With the exception of a gnarled retainer, keen to point out the more interesting features of the structure for a small consideration, you may well find yourself alone there. Cannons peep out from bracken-covered battlements, and the church bell rocks gently in the breeze; at any second, you almost expect Fernando de Castro to come galloping past with his Portuguese army to do battle for the castle all over again. Strategically situated almost on the frontier with Portugal, Monterrey not surprisingly featured prominently in the Spanish-Portuguese wars of the 14th century.

It was a town as much as a simple castle, for within its heavily fortified walls it contained a monastery, a hospital and a variety of houses. It was the first town in Galicia to have its own printing press, and it was in Monterrey that the Millal of Auria, famous throughout Spain, was printed in 1494.

If your nerves are strong, you can make the hairy climb to the top of the 15th-century keep and an even hairier ascent up the 14th-century Lady's Tower. Best of all is the 13th-century church with a splendid portal, a marvellous carved altar and a fine set of figures depicting the Annunciation.

▶ Nearby

Orense NW, 70km by road. A sprawling new town spreads out from the interesting old centre, which was originally developed around the natural hot water that emerges from three springs at a temperature of 65°C. Worth seeing are the cathedral (particularly its Paradise Door), the Roman Bridge and the Archaeological and Fine Arts Museum, with a fine 17th-century carving of the Stations of the Cross.

Alto de Covelo To the north-east of Verín, the twin east-west highways N120 and N525 are linked by a minor road from Freixido to la Gudiña – the C533 – which takes you through glorious scenery. Travelling southward, the road rises gently through vineyards and forests – at grape-harvest time in October, the roads are full of horses and carts, loaded with glistening black grapes. Higher up towards the pass of Alto de Covelo (1052m), the views become truly spectacular. Tiny villages of houses with large tiled roofs, clustered together among huge terraces of vines; hundreds and hundreds of sweet chestnut trees; butterflies of all colours swarming around an abundance of wild flowers. As the road winds down, the scenery is enhanced by several large reservoirs.

The castle of Monterrey from the Parador.

▶ Where to stay

Parador Nacional Monterrey £££ ☎ 988 410075 According to Conrad Hilton, only three things matter when it comes to building a hotel: location, location and location. In that case, this Parador must be rated one of the best, since it has one of the finest settings in all Spain. Opened in 1965, its exterior was designed to mirror Monterrey castle opposite. The bedrooms are large, with wide use of natural wood, and offer mini-bars and direct-dial telephones; the views from the rooms are excellent. Unusually for a Parador, it also has a swimming pool – topped up with ice-cold water which only the British appear hardy enough, or foolhardy enough, to brave.

The food ranks among the best to be found in the Paradores of Northern Spain; the local specialities – *caldo gallego* (hot soup with white beans and cabbage) and the *filloas* dessert (pancakes filled with custard) – are particularly recommended.

Alternatives An hour's drive to the east along the N525 is Puebla de Sanabria, on the edge of our area, which also has a Parador (£££ ☎ 988 620001). We haven't inspected it, but our plea for feedback from readers of the first edition was answered with uniformly approving reports: 'Nice bedroom and super bathroom, with the best shower in Spain!' Mrs J A S Verrill; 'Nice rooms, quiet' Dr Michael Tarsh.

■ VILLAFRANCA DEL BIERZO

Some towns, it seems, acquire a Parador through their outstanding merits as a tourist attraction – Santillana del Mar, for example; others have a Parador thrust upon them for no particularly obvious reason. On the face of things Villafranca del Bierzo falls into the latter category. It has a Romanesque church or two, and a 15th-century castle; good, but really only par for the course in this part of Spain. Why bother putting the place on your itinerary? There are three reasons why you might.

First, Villafranca is plumb in the middle of a yawning gap between the highlights of the central and western parts of Northern Spain. Secondly, the Parador staff are among the most welcoming and efficient of any that we met. And thirdly, Villafranca is itself attractive in an unspectacular sort of way. We wouldn't go quite as far as the Parador's promotional leaflet, which describes Villafranca as 'the Promised Land, the Eden, the Paradise of the plain, majestic and impressive as it lies surrounded by mountain'. But it does lie in a very attractive spot, between the mountain passes of El Manzanal and Piedrafita del Cebrero, overlooking the plain towards Ponferrada.

The biggest attraction of the town is its complete naturalness; nothing is self-consciously arranged for the tourist; there are no folkloric dances, no people dressed in funny hats. This is rural Spain, take it or leave it. See the 'official' guide-book attractions (particularly the Romanesque church), but above all enjoy the town for what it is. Its network of cobbled streets and alleyways conceals large houses bearing their coats of arms and nestling behind spacious courtyards, while squeezed into any remaining spaces are tiny houses, with wrought iron balconies garlanded with flowers. In some ways it is the equal of Santillana del Mar; but while Santillana has a stage-set Disneyland quality, Villafranca is undeniably the real thing. Its dimly-lit shops sell locally made wine and beer, or bottles of locally grown cherries and pimentos; the smell of newly-made bread fills the morning air; at the Friday morning market you appear to be able to buy anything from fish to figs and sweet chestnuts.

On a balmy October afternoon, we were lingering outside a vineyard near the castle when two women, passing by with a huge flask of grape juice, noticed us. They knew at once we were visitors, and ran into the vineyard to cut down two bunches of fat, juicy black grapes which they offered to us with smiles and good wishes before going on to continue with the grape harvest in a nearby field.

▶ Nearby

Ponferrada SE, 25km by road. It has to be admitted that this is not one of the prettiest cities in Northern Spain. Its main attraction is an extremely beautiful turreted castle built by the Knights Templar to offer refuge to pilgrims on their way to Santiago de Compostela. Pilgrims might have paused here, but there's no reason why you should.

▶ Where to stay

Parador Nacional de Villafranca del Bierzo ££ ☎ 987 540175
When we visited this hotel in 1985 we were impressed by the warmth of its staff and its agreeable location, but not by its decorative state. We understand that it has since been refurbished, but we have not yet been back. Reports from readers would be very welcome.

■ VILLALBA

When the British day-dream, we talk of building castles in the air. When the French day-dream, they talk of building castles in Spain. The quantity and variety of castles still to be seen in Spain suggests that day-dreaming has been taking place on a prodigious scale. But very few of the ancient castles which are dotted around Northern Spain have been converted into Paradores, and in our western area there is only one – that of Villalba. The Parador is housed in a magnificent octagonal medieval fortress right in the middle of the town. The stout walls, the drawbridge which you still have to cross to enter the hotel, and the tiny slit windows indicate that this is no sham castle but played a crucial role in the control of this area of Galicia.

Villalba itself is a pleasant enough town, except that it is uncomfortably bisected by the main road, which seems to be used by an excessive number of heavy lorries (excessive even for Spain). This makes the main streets of Villalba an unpleasant place to linger, and discourages visitors from staying more than a night. Which is a pity, because we have the feeling that there are some pleasant excursions to be enjoyed in the nearby countryside, even if it holds no great historical treasures (apart from Lugo). We'd like to hear from anyone who has had the time to investigate Villalba and its environs, and who can offer some suggestions for worthwhile local jaunts.

One thing we did try was one of the locally produced conical San Simon cheeses which are a sort of Galician Gouda and exceptionally toothsome.

▶ Nearby

Lugo S, 35km by road. The city's most striking asset is the solid granite walls which still encircle the centre – and through which you can pass only by one of a small number of gates. The walls have existed since Roman times, and have suffered at the hands of various advancing and retreating armies. They form a continuous perimeter of over 1km and have a height of 10 metres, and you can walk around the city on top of them.

As a stop on the Pilgrims' Way to Santiago de Compostela, you would expect Lugo to have a beanfeast of a cathedral; you would not be disappointed. It's been tinkered with and modified over the centuries and has picked up something from most architectural styles. The most affecting aspect of the cathedral is the Chapel of the Virgin with Big Eyes, with its remarkable Baroque rotunda. The interior of the cathedral has a Romanesque nave and large wooden Renaissance altar-pieces. A few minutes from the cathedral is the provincial museum, which includes a reconstruction of a typical kitchen found in a local country cottage. Also worth savouring are the old streets with their wrought iron balconies. It's probably not a place to stay, although there is an acceptable four-star hotel (Hotel-Residencia Lugo-Husa – reports please!), but a place to stop and enjoy en route to somewhere else – it lies conveniently at the heart of Galicia at the crossroads of routes to La Coruña, Orense, Ribadeo and León.

Parador Nacional Condes de Villalba

▶ Where to stay

Parador Nacional Condes de Villalba £££ ☎ 982 510011 The castle was converted into a hotel in 1967, and the task was carried out splendidly. The rooms are absolutely enormous, with wooden floors and ceilings, stone fire-places and antique furnishings. The main reception hall is cavernous, with a massive arched ceiling, and the walls decorated with medieval wall hangings.

The First Law of Paradores, which holds that the friendliness of the staff diminishes in inverse ratio to the quality of the establishment, doesn't hold good here. When the water failed during our stay, due to a drop in pressure, solicitous staff laid on a continuous supply of jugs of water for washing.

A night spent here is, in its own way, every bit as exciting as a night spent at the Los Reyes Católicos in Santiago or the San Marcos in León. The hotel has only six bedrooms, so if you plan to stay here during the peak summer months you will probably need to book well in advance.

The Centre

Wild Spain; rugged mountains still roamed by wolves and bears, where wild flowers abound. Smart Spain with prosperous towns like Burgos and Oviedo, and resorts like Gijón and Santander. And, best of all perhaps, León with its magnificent cathedral and luxury hotel.

BASES IN THE CENTRE

We have divided Northern Spain into three: the West, the Centre and the East. In each area we have sifted out those villages, towns or cities which you will probably want to use as a base – because there are interesting sights or good hotels to be found there.

Each base is the subject of a separate short chapter which provides a brief account of the place as a whole, followed by details of the sights you should see, the attractions that can be found in places nearby, the hotel or hotels where you should stay – and alternative accommodation you might consider if rooms don't happen to be available in our selected hotels. We have also included, where appropriate, comments from holidaymakers who have completed questionnaires distributed by Brittany Ferries and from readers who have taken the first edition of the guide with them on holiday in Northern Spain.

These are our bases in the Centre:

Hotel prices are indicated by ratings. In 1987, prices for a double room with bath are roughly as follows:

£	under £20
££	£20 to £30
£££	£30 to £40
££££	£40 to £55
£££££	£55 to £75

INTRODUCTION

The heart of Northern Spain and, in many ways, its most beautiful part. Certainly the rugged scenery of the Picos de Europa, with its plunging valleys and deep gorges, offers some of the finest views to be seen in Europe. There are lush forests, a colourful array of wild flowers and all manner of wild-life, from wolves and bears to vultures and eagles.

There are delightful seaside towns with quiet beaches, and bigger resorts like Gijón or the ferry port of Santander, which offers a casino and a variety of smart shops and elegant restaurants. An hour's drive from Santander is the delightful village of Santillana del Mar which is unchanged from the times when the fictional hero Gil Blas is supposed to have lived there: grand noblemen's houses overlook delightful narrow, cobbled streets along which cows are driven every morning and evening, as they have been for hundreds of years.

This area is rich in history. It was here, near Oviedo, that the fight to reconquer Spain from the Moorish invaders began in 722 when a small but significant defeat was inflicted against them in Covadonga, a marvellous spot in the foothills of the Picos. Oviedo has played a significant part throughout Spanish history. The country's capital for a short time at the start of the Reconquest, it was at the centre of events during the turbulent years of the thirties because of the unrest among the miners of the surrounding Asturian coal-fields. Further inland the scenery becomes mellower and the weather hotter. The countryside around León is scorched. The city itself is a visual feast; from the magical stained glass of the cathedral to the exuberant façade of the Hostal San Marcos, once a medieval hospital but now one of the finest hotels in the world. Like León, Burgos (in the south-east corner of this area) was an important staging post on the Pilgrims' Way to Santiago – and it too has a spectacular cathedral, plus a supporting cast of other worthwhile sights to see.

If on your motoring holiday you never venture outside this central region, you will have more than enough to keep you busy and happily enthralled.

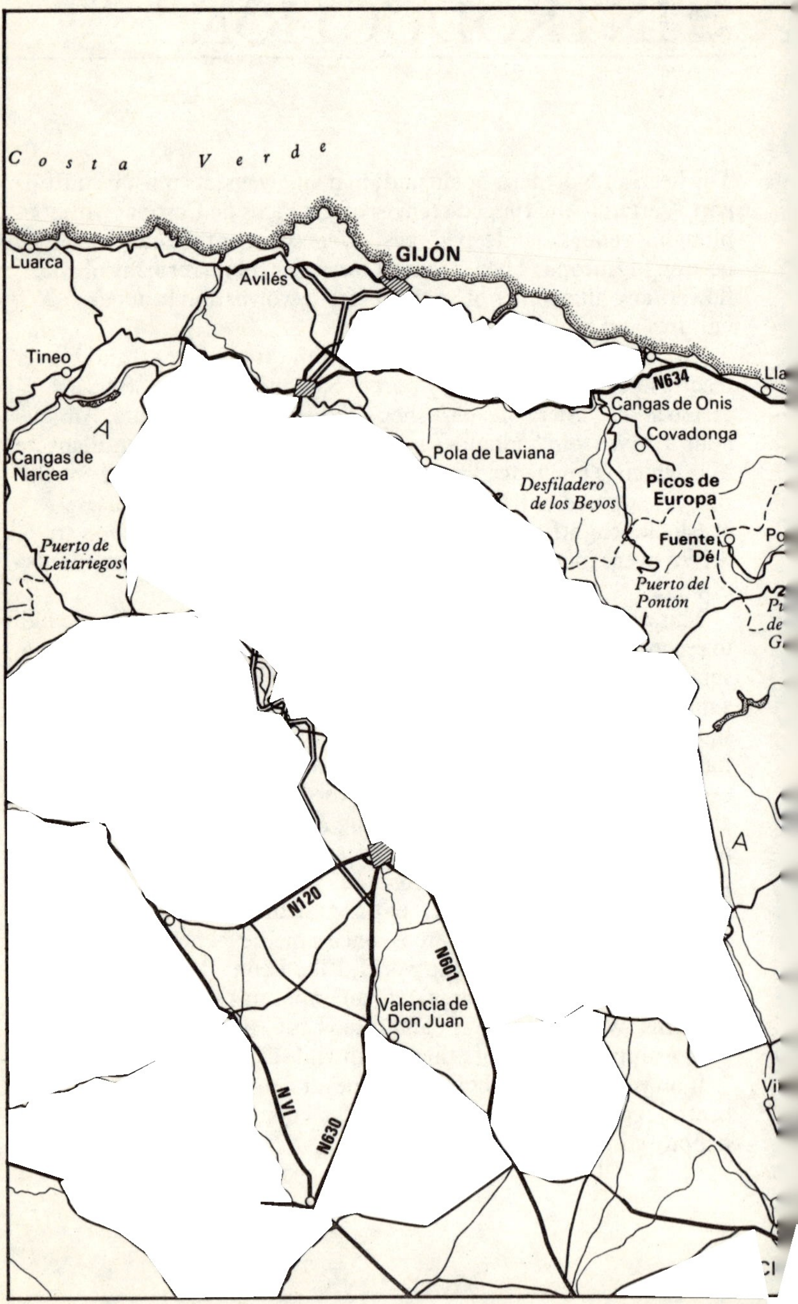
Costa Verde
GIJÓN
Luarca
Avilés
Tineo
N634
Cangas de Onis
Covadonga
Pola de Laviana
Cangas de Narcea
Desfiladero de los Beyos
Picos de Europa
Puerto de Leitariegos
Fuente Dé
Puerto del Pontón
N120
N601
Valencia de Don Juan
N VI
N630

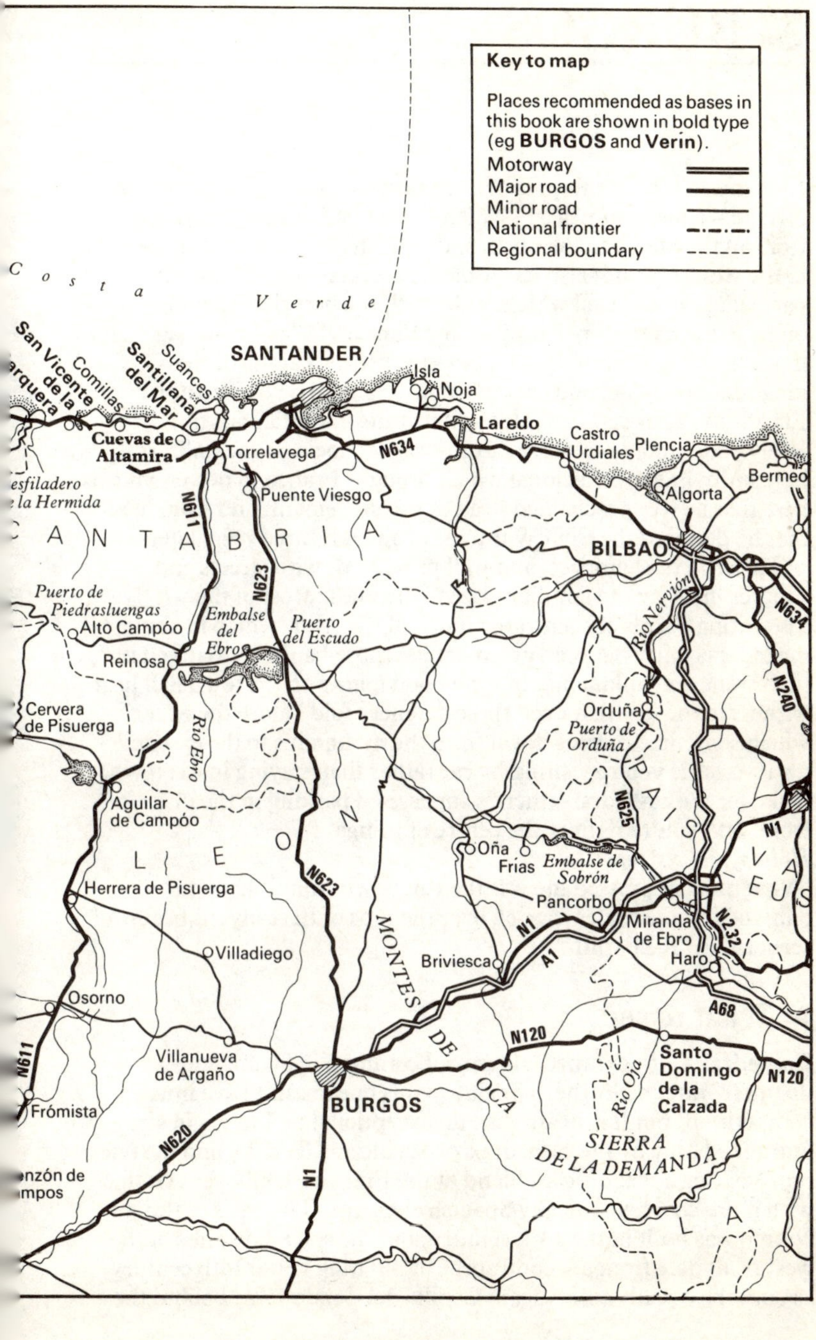
Key to map
Places recommended as bases in this book are shown in bold type (eg BURGOS and Verín).
Motorway
Major road
Minor road
National frontier
Regional boundary
Costa Verde
SANTANDER
Santillana del Mar
Suances
Comillas
San Vicente de la Barquera
Cuevas de Altamira
Torrelavega
Isla
Noja
Laredo
Castro Urdiales
Plencia
Bermeo
Algorta
BILBAO
Puente Viesgo
CANTABRIA
Puerto de Piedrasluengas
Alto Campóo
Embalse del Ebro
Puerto del Escudo
Reinosa
Cervera de Pisuerga
Río Ebro
Aguilar de Campóo
LEON
Herrera de Pisuerga
Villadiego
Osorno
Villanueva de Argaño
Frómista
BURGOS
MONTES DE OCA
Oña
Frías
Embalse de Sobrón
Pancorbo
Briviesca
Miranda de Ebro
Haro
Orduña
Puerto de Orduña
Río Nervión
PAIS VASCO
Santo Domingo de la Calzada
Río Oja
SIERRA DE LA DEMANDA
N611
N623
N634
N625
N240
N1
A1
N232
A68
N120
N620

■ BURGOS

Like most cities in this part of the world, Burgos is prosperous and relaxed – a pleasant place in which to stay. What distinguishes it from all the others to the north and east (though not from those to the west) is that it also has some spectacular sightseeing – in particular, a cathedral which ranks with the best that Spain has to offer. Burgos was very firmly on the Pilgrims' Way to Santiago, and it has its own claims to fame. It was briefly the capital of the kingdom of Castile, and can just about claim to be the birthplace of El Cid, the 11th-century soldier of fortune made famous by Hollywood; more recently, Burgos was the focus of the military-based Movimiento Nacional which brought Franco to power – it was here that he was proclaimed head of the movement, and from here that he declared the Civil War to be at an end, three years later.

The centre is compact, and well preserved, with streets and squares lined by the familiar glazed balconies. Most of the interesting part is concentrated north of the river, which in summer meanders gently between green banks; those banks are flanked by high stone embankments, but the flood marks on the town hall bear witness to the fact that even these defences fold before the water which sometimes comes down from the mountains to the east and north-east. If you're visiting by car rather than staying in the town, make for the cathedral – there's supervised parking in the plaza in front, and you're right at the centre of things.

Holidaymakers' reports

'What most impressed me was the run down from Burgos to Santander – the eagles soaring over the tops of the canyon; beautiful scenery' E J R Bentliff

▶ What to see

Cathedral Gothic cathedrals are not common in Spain, and distinctly rare in Northern Spain, so this one doesn't have much competition; but it is in any case an exceptional building – in size outranked only by the cathedrals of Seville and Toledo, and in style representing a magnificent blend of the French Flamboyant Gothic with more characteristically Spanish elements. The basis of the church was built in the 13th century, but the splendid spires of the west front date from a second surge of building in the 15th century, as does the equally extravagant Capilla del Condestable behind the altar. The cathedral is full of interest, from the grand central lantern above the transept crossing to the tomb of El Cid directly beneath it. Unusual features include the majestic Escalera Dorada, a double staircase leading up to the north door, and the 16th-century *Pampamoscas* ('fly-catcher') clock, with a grotesque, brightly painted human figure which opens its mouth on the striking of the hour. Because the cathedral is built on a hillside, you can get a good close-up view of its intricate exterior stonework by walking around on its north side.

Arco de Santa María Just south of the cathedral, this is a vestige of the city's fortifications, facing the river bridge of the same name. Although the arch dates from the 11th century, the statuary in which it is now clothed is of 16th-century origin.

Casa del Cordón A couple of hundred yards east of the cathedral, across the pleasant oval space of the Plaza José Antonio, is this historic palace – so named because of the Franciscan cord embellishment on the façade. It was here that Ferdinand and Isabella (los Reyes Católicos) received Columbus on returning from his second trip to America. The palace is currently being restored.

San Nicolás This church, close to the west front of the cathedral, has a remarkable altarpiece which was carved at the beginning of the 16th century and contains all sorts of interesting scenes.

Casa de Miranda This fine mansion now houses the local archaeological museum, which contains several objects of more than local interest.

▶ Nearby

Cartuja de Miraflores A short drive east on the south side of the river brings you through woods to this 15th-century monastery. Its church was completed by Isabella the Catholic, and its centrepiece is an elaborate memorial to her parents, Juan II and Isabel of Portugal, with carving of astonishing intricacy.

Monasterio de las Huelgas This Cistercian nunnery just west of the centre was based on a royal rural retreat (*huelga* means 'rest') and admitted only the very best young ladies. It became a place of enormous power in the 13th and 14th centuries – Edward I was knighted here, as well as many Castilian kings – and now offers interesting guided tours (in Spanish and French only, at least when we visited) of grand rooms in various styles, including arabic Mujedar decoration. There is a fine Romanesque cloister and the chapterhouse, draped with historic flags and tent-flaps, has

The cathedral, framed by glazed balconies

interesting columns made up of several separate stone shafts. The great novelty of the church is a pivoted pulpit, designed to allow the preacher to lecture either the nuns or the public. There is a famous and unique collection of medieval textiles and other finds from royal tombs; sadly it was closed when we visited.

▶ Where to stay

Landa Palace ££££ ☎ 947 206343 The Landa Palace is without doubt the best hotel in town, except that it isn't in town at all – it's a couple of miles south. That in itself is a drawback, since Burgos (more than most cities) is a place you're likely to want to stay in rather than near; what's more, the setting is unappealing – on high ground, exposed but without remarkable views, and close to the busy Madrid highway. But there are compensations: the hotel is based on a squat, solid tower dating from the 14th century which now accommodates the grand entrance hall and above that the King of Spain's suite; the rest of the hotel is architecturally more ordinary, but the whole is superbly furnished in grand style, and the atmosphere is at once welcoming but dignified. There is a splendid indoor swimming pool, and another pool in the garden.

Alternatives In the city, the most distinctive hotel is the Mesón del Cid (££ ☎ 947 205971), in a slightly elevated spot right opposite the west front of the cathedral; it is traditional in style, and spick-and-span throughout. The Mesón del Cid faces competition from two conventional upmarket city-centre hotels, both of them housed in modern (but not *very* modern) buildings of no great distinction. The better buy is the Condestable (££ ☎ 947 205740), just to the east of the central area – it is spacious and comfortable, with traditional-style restaurant and bar, and a stylish cafeteria; we have one favourable report: 'Very good service and attention' John Hallett. The Almirante Bonifaz (£££ ☎ 947 206943), a little further east, is glossier but a bit less welcoming.

Simpler and less spacious hotels offer some savings. The Fernán González (££ ☎ 947 209441) is neat and quite comfortable, with a mix of modern and traditional styles; it is south of the river, but still quite central. The Corona de Castilla (££ ☎ 947 262142), further south, costs much the same and is less appealing. The Cordón (££ ☎ 947 265000) is a refreshing change – coolly stylish décor in an old town-house close to the centre – but when we visited was surrounded by building works (including the restoration of the historic Casa del Cordón) which rather interfered with the ambience.

■ GIJÓN

Like several otherwise generally unremarkable places in Northern Spain, Gijón (pronounced 'Hee-hawn' like a donkey's bray) has been blessed with a Parador and so demands attention. Gijón's Parador is newly built; four years after its opening, it still smells and feels new (and like all new places, it has doors that won't shut and windows that won't open!).

But why a Parador in Gijón? Certainly it's an attractive enough place with its wide, sweeping San Lorenzo beach pounded by huge Atlantic breakers (and a beach packed as tight as Blackpool's at the height of the season). It's also one of Spain's most important ports, with a massive coaling harbour at El Mussel. It also has its place in history and the arts as the birthplace of the 18th-century reformer and man of letters, Jovellanos.

But the real reason why Gijón has been singled out for the Parador treatment is to be found in the sports ground next door to the hotel. The large El Molinono sports stadium (home ground of First Division football club Sporting Gijón) staged one of the groups of the 1982 World Cup Finals (a brass plaque in the hotel's gardens bears the engraved signatures of the German, Austrian, Algerian and Chilean teams who took part). So the powers that be favoured Gijón with a Parador, and a jolly good one it is too (despite the recalcitrant doors and windows).

Gijón, in the words of Michelin, might not be worth a detour. But en route to or from Santander it will provide a welcoming stop-off point – particularly if you've been following the tortuous road along the coast from Ribadeo and Luarca. If you need somewhere to jog off the tensions of driving, the Parador is next door to an excellent park, complete with a fitness trail for adults and children, and a selection of animals including a collection of noisy peacocks.

This is one city where you will be glad if you've invested in a copy of the Michelin Red Guide to Spain: its street map is indispensable when it comes to finding your way through Gijón's maze of streets.

► What to see

Gijón yields up one or two sights of interest. The old fishermen's quarter clusters around the hill at Santa Catalina (that's an old quarter rather than old fishermen, although there appeared to be a few of those in evidence too). Among the bars and restaurants here, you will find the Museo Casa-Natal de Jovellanos, which as well as revealing some fine wooden carving and a number of good paintings by local artists, will show you what a period Spanish house looks like inside, with a glazed courtyard and a classic Spanish fireplace.

▶ Nearby

Villaviciosa SE, 30km by road. An interesting town full of Romanesque architecture. Emperor Charles V landed here in 1517 to claim his kingdom, thinking he'd arrived at Santander. While the local townspeople were surprised and delighted at this unexpected arrival, it appears that the future King of Spain was less than pleased at the error in map-reading.

▶ Where to stay

Parador Nacional El Molino Viejo £££ ☎ 985 370511 There would have to be a very good reason for staying anywhere else in Gijón. The central core of the hotel, containing the bar and the dining room, is modelled on an old Asturian water-mill. The bedroom blocks, while modern in style, are elegantly and extremely tastefully furnished: large bedrooms with varnished, wooden floors, comfortable settees, polished wooden desks and smart brass lamps, colour TVs, radios and direct dial telephones. And even by the normal standards of the Paradores, the Gijón breakfast would rate a thumbs up from Billy Bunter: on top of the standard fare come Spanish omelettes, fresh fruit salad and hot toast.

Holidaymakers' reports

'Well appointed: superb bedrooms and facilities; not easy to find without a map' Jean Boxall, Doreen Gascoigne

'Excellent all round' Mr Mason

'Good rooms and food' R H W Jones

'Must rank in the Top Ten' Jim Matthews

Alternatives There are two other good hotels in the town: the Príncipe de Asturias (££££ ☎ 985 367111), a cosy friendly hotel right on the beach with excellent views of the sea, and the Hernán Cortés (££ ☎ 985 346000), which is also perfectly acceptable.

■ LAREDO

Laredo is the nearest thing you'll find on the coast of Northern Spain to the big beach resorts of the Mediterranean costas; but by costa standards it is quiet and dignified, with very little of the brashness of Benidorm, and its glorious, long sweep of a beach is backed mainly by apartment blocks rather than hotels. It may not be the sort of resort most readers of this book will be travelling in search of – but for a few days on the beach it offers a worthwhile compromise between the smartness of San Sebastián and the simplicity of many other places to the west. Most of the resort stretches along a broad spit of sand which has built up at the mouth of the Río Asón; across the river mouth, at first glance seeming to be joined to the beach, is the imposing 1000-foot bulk of Monte Ganzo, sheltering the bay and the fishing port of Santoña from the full force of the Atlantic waves.

▶ What to see

Old quarter At the extreme eastern end of Laredo's magnificent bay is the original town – a jumble of narrow, old, atmospheric streets climbing steeply to the 13th-century church of Nuestra Señora de la Asunción. There is also a 16th-century Ayuntamiento and other fine houses to be seen.

▶ Nearby

Noja NW, 25km by road. Laredo doesn't have a local monopoly of fine beaches, and at several points along the indented coastline to the north-west, around the little village of Noja, there are small resorts with hotels, campsites and apartments to rent. See 'Where to stay'.

Castro Urdiales E, 25km by road. This small resort and fishing port makes an interesting and pleasant place to pause. It has a splendid setting, with its long beach curling around to culminate in a small and colourful harbour at the foot of a steep headland, whereon sit the 14th-century church of Santa Maria and the ruins of a castle of the Knights Templar. There are neat gardens on the prom, pavement cafés, and a backdrop of rugged hills. The N634 between Laredo and Castro Urdiales is at its most tortuous, and overtaking the heavy lorries you are sure to encounter is both difficult and pointless; fortunately, the scenery along the way is splendid.

ayona
arador Conde de Gondomar
swimming Pool ₽40-55

---

nonterray (Castle)
Parador Nacional Monterrey
Swimming Pool ₽30-40

---

illafranca
arador Villafranca del Bierzo
₽20-30

---

illalba
arador Nacional Condes de Villalba
₽30-40
No Chance unless booked

Leon

San Marcos Hostal

£40 - 55

Asón valley The Río Asón leads off into some splendid mountain scenery south of Laredo, where you could spend days and weeks exploring. Near Ramales de la Victoria are the caves of Covalanas, which have important prehistoric cave-paintings.

▶ Where to stay

El Ancla £££ ☎ 942 605500 'The Anchor' is well placed for access to both the huge beach and the old town of Laredo, and is a very pleasant small hotel. It is in a quiet residential street just back from the beach, surrounded by villas and gardens. Its own garden is not huge, but attractively green and shady (there are some rooms directly off this area). For a small place the lobby is quite grand, and there is a comfortably furnished, airy lounge.

Alternatives In the same quiet, leafy street as El Ancla, but with rather less style, is the cheaper El Cortijo (£ ☎ 942 605600). Not far away to the west, on the road backing the beach, is the Cosmopol (££ ☎ 942 605400) – a functional but adequate modern block. We have

Low tide at Playa de Isla

good reports of the Riscó (££ ☎ 942 605030), in a fine position up the hill behind the town: 'Excellent food' Mr Moreau; 'Modern, clean, quiet' Mr & Mrs W B Huelsman. At Playa de Isla (also known as Quejo) there are good sandy beaches and several small hotels; the two-star Astuy (££ ☎ 942 630250) enjoys the best position, with a terrace overlooking a small rocky cove, and is simple but neat in style. At low tide, the beach to the west stretches (barring the odd stream) round to join Playa de Ris – a splendid dune-backed strand with big, well organised campsites on the sandy flat land behind, as well as a few hotels and apartment blocks.

■ LEÓN

By the time you reach León on your drive through Northern Spain, you will have learned that first impressions can be misleading. To judge by the first sight of its outskirts, León is like any other modern Spanish city: a few smoke-belching factories and a crop of ugly apartment blocks. But as you move nearer to the older heart of the city, there is an increasing sense of excitement: you begin to realise that you are on the threshold of something special. You may catch a glimpse of the cathedral, you may take a wrong turning (no – you will almost certainly take a wrong turning!) and find yourself nosing up a tiny one-way street past ancient houses and through marvellous arcaded squares that are reminiscent of Venice.

If you are lucky, your ultimate destination in León will be the San Marcos Hostal, a hotel that will take your breath away with its serene magnificence. But whether you're staying or simply passing through, your visit to León will be one to treasure.

▶ What to see

Cathedral When the guide-books compare León cathedral to Chartres, it sounds a little too much like journalistic hyperbole. León's cathedral might be impressive, but as good as Chartres – surely not? At first glimpse, the cathedral cannot match Chartres' massive airship-hangar bulk. But once through the remarkable portals, the point of the comparison becomes clear.

The stained-glass windows produce a breathtaking swirl of colour. The guide-books tell you that the cathedral has 125 windows and 57 oculi producing an area of glass totalling 1,200 square metres – in fact, so much glass and so little wall that the cathedral is in danger of collapsing. But nothing can prepare you for their full dramatic effect. León cathedral is unique in Spain, for its windows as much as for its clean-cut elegance. We were fortunate enough to attend an evening concert in the cathedral, a performance of works by Handel and Bach. During Bach's Brandenburg Concerto No. 1, the lights in the cathedral were turned out and the outside spotlights turned on, flooding the inside of the building with a blaze of stained-glass colour so sensational that the audience simply gasped.

Holidaymakers' reports

'Very moving: possibly the high-point of our visit' S & M Jenkins

Basilica of San Isidoro San Isidoro is built into the old city walls, an impressive chunk of which can still be seen behind the basilica. The Royal Pantheon and Treasury, whose entrance is to the left of the church, contain some exceptional 12th-century frescoes illustrating New Testament, hunting and pastoral scenes. According to Michelin, the capitals show 'profane boxing scenes and grotesques', but we couldn't find them nor would the exceptionally proper lady guide point them out to us – perhaps you might have better luck.

San Marcos Monastery The magnificent 100-metre façade of San Marcos Monastery barely prepares you for its even more astonishing interior. As this is the best hotel in León and certainly one of the five best in Spain, there is more to be said of this later; suffice to say that even if you aren't fortunate enough to stay here, you should certainly visit San Marcos both to enjoy its sumptuous elegance and to see the small but touchingly beautiful 11th-century ivory Carrizo Crucifix displayed in the archaeological museum.

▶ Nearby

Puerto de Pajares N, 60km by road. For those driving south to León from Oviedo, the build-up is suitably dramatic, particularly if you have elected to forgo the comforts of the motorway and instead take the old road up through the Pajares pass. Happily the motorway seems to have filtered off the heavy traffic, leaving the mountain drive free and easy for the tourist.

The early stages from Oviedo take you through rough, untidy coal-mining areas, where mighty slag-heaps and dark satanic mills scar the countryside. (It's remarkably similar to the Welsh mining valleys.) But after leaving Campomanes, the road begins to climb into the mountains, offering spectacular views at every turn. During the autumn, when the sweet chestnuts, ash and oak trees change colour, the lower slopes of the hills are ablaze with red and gold.

At the very top of the Pajares pass (1379m) stands a Parador, closed down and looking sadly forlorn now that it's by-passed by the motorway; but you can park here and look back down the road you have just climbed, and over the jumble of mountain peaks. The drive down the other side of the mountains towards León is quick and easy. The change in the countryside is striking; the verdant hills are now replaced by scorched wheat fields. Even when the weather on the Oviedo side is overcast and chilly, here the sun may be burning hot.

Astorga SW, 50km by road. The next major stop after León for the pilgrims on their way to Santiago de Compostela, Astorga was well known for the excellence of its fairs. Set in pretty, verdant countryside, the city is worth visiting for its cathedral and a bizarre episcopal palace, which looks like Sleeping Beauty's castle and was built in 1889 by Antonio Gaudi, best known for his outstanding architectural work in Barcelona. The town is also famous for the Maragatos people who live in the surrounding countryside; they are a reclusive race believed to be descended from Berbers and Visigoths – you may be fortunate enough to see some in the town dressed in their distinctive costume (men in baggy trousers and women in brightly coloured shawls and full skirts).

San Marcos

Valporquero Caves N, 35km by road. Dramatic formations of stalactites – including a stalactite star; all stained an extraordinary variety of colours and tones by the mineral oxides in the stone.

▶ Where to stay

San Marcos Hostal ££££ ☎ 987 237300 Unless you're exceptionally well informed on these things, you probably won't have heard of León's San Marcos hotel. Once you've seen it, you're unlikely ever to forget it. Its official category is five-star *grande luxe* and Michelin gives it a rating of five red gables – and this in an area where any red rating is noteworthy. Classifications and categorisations are pitifully inadequate when it comes to conveying the attraction of the San Marcos. One writer describes it as one of the five best hotels in the world. You would have to agree with that; but the San Marcos is more than simply a hotel, it is an experience – for a night or two you are allowed to indulge yourself in magnificence.

There may be some hotels that offer greater luxury than the San Marcos; there are few that can match it for style and grandeur. The core of the hotel is a 12th-century monastery where soldier friars helped protect pilgrims on the way to Santiago de Compostela. (The hotel's chambermaids are dressed in what look like nurses' uniforms, presumably in the tradition of the hotel's role as a pilgrim's hospital.) The foyer is a large hall decorated with paintings and other art treasures; large windows reveal delightful cloisters filled with sculptures and a variety of Roman archaeological discoveries.

Holidaymakers' reports

'Simply sensational' Colin Morgan

'Outstanding value for money' Mr Michaels

'Make every effort to stay at this extraordinary hotel; we only stayed a night, we wish we had stayed a fortnight!' Mrs Playfair

'All you say about it is true' Dr Michael Tarsh

Alternatives Going to León without staying at the San Marcos would be an eminently unsatisfying experience, rather like having strawberries without cream. But there are other good hotels – principally the excellent four-star Conde Luna (££ ☎ 987 206512), situated in the heart of the city a few minutes' walk from the cathedral; and the Quindós (£ ☎ 987 236200), a few minutes' walk from the San Marcos.

■ OVIEDO

Once you get to Oviedo, says the latest tourism campaign of the capital of Asturias, just see if you can leave it. What they mean, of course, is that once you become familiar with Oviedo's smart shops and its sophisticated way of life, you'll find it very difficult to tear yourself away from it all. Unfortunately, at the same time that the city came up with its catchy little slogan Oviedo introduced a one-way system of mind-boggling complexity. Now people are not only finding it very difficult to leave Oviedo – it takes a mighty effort of the intellect to steer your way into its centre in the first place.

Oviedo has played a major role in Spanish life for over a thousand years. It was nearby in Covadonga that the fight to reconquer Spain from the Moors achieved its first victory in 722. Alfonso II subsequently established his court in Oviedo, making it the capital of Asturias, and the city remained the centre of the Spanish struggle against the Moors until 910. (The special importance of Asturias to the Spanish kingdom is illustrated by the fact that the elder son of the monarch is given the title of Prince of Asturias.)

At the heart of the Asturian coal-fields, Oviedo has also featured prominently in Spain's recent turbulent political history. In October 1934, revolutionary miners attempted to seize control of the city. A violent battle with the regular army followed; as you can see today, the cathedral was particularly badly damaged and its Camara Santa, the 'Holy Room' which houses the cathedral's precious relics and priceless treasures, blown up. Later, when Civil War broke out in Spain, the city was split by the conflict, and again badly damaged.

Today, Oviedo is one of the smartest and most prosperous of the cities in Northern Spain. The city's beautiful people who gather in the lobby of the Hotel de la Reconquista for pre-dinner cocktails arrive in silver Porsches and wear elegant designer clothes.

Oviedo has good road links with Santander to the east and León to the south (which can now be reached by motorway), making the city a convenient stopping-off point. The road west to Luarca and Ribadeo is absolutely appalling, and should be avoided if possible.

▶ What to see

Cathedral A blackened edifice that looks much the worse for wear after the damage it suffered in various periods of civil strife during the 1930s. Its most splendid treasure is the Arca Santa, the Cross of

Victory situated in the Camara Santa (faithfully rebuilt following its destruction in 1934).

Old city There are some fine old buildings and squares near the cathedral, particularly the cathedral square, Plaza de Daoiz y Velarde, where the market is held daily, and the Plaza de Porlier.

▶ Nearby

Covadonga E, 85km by road. A landmark of immense importance in Spanish history. It was here, in the foothills of the mighty Picos de Europa, that the Moors met their first defeat in around 722, at the hands of tribal leader Pelayo (see page 15). This success provided the impetus for the Reconquest of Christian Spain from the Muslim invaders. Covadonga is in a beautiful wooded spot dwarfed by mountains all around. It is quickly reached from the main N634 Oviedo to Santander road, through Cangas de Onis – which is also a pleasant little town with a marvellous old hump-backed bridge and a bustling Sunday-morning market.

An horreo – common in Asturias and all points west

▶ Where to stay

Hotel de la Reconquista ££££ ☎ 985 241100 This is an excellent hotel which stands comparison with the San Marcos in León or Los Reyes Católicos in Santiago. Like these two other illustrious hotels, the Hotel de la Reconquista was originally built during the reigns of Ferdinand VI and Charles III as a hospice and hospital – now only the magnificent façade of the original building remains. Inside, however, the hotel is elegant and tremendously refined – in the public rooms there are some fine modern paintings by local artists.
Holidaymakers' reports
'Luxury hotel exuding an impressively opulent air. In need of a good cleaning – carpets, walls stained slightly – ragged round edges' John & Geraldine McCaughrean

Alternatives If you can't get a room at the Hotel de la Reconquista, Gijón, about 15 minutes away by motorway, has the best alternatives (see page 76); but in Oviedo La Jirafa (££ ☎ 985 222244) is highly recommended by two travellers: 'La Jirafa is first rate! We arrived very late at 11.30pm – they dealt with us beautifully, supplying ice with mineral water; good lighting and courteous staff' M Rosenberg & L Kilpatrick

■ PICOS DE EUROPA

Northern Spain is a predominantly mountainous area – across the whole breadth of the country is a band of high ground which is never less than rugged, and often positively wild. It is at its most extreme in the Picos de Europa, which may not equal the Alps in scale – they reach only 2600 metres – but which are more than a match in grandeur and scenic drama. What's more they are easily accessible, and not the exclusive preserve of the mountaineer: only 30km inland, and a little over two hours' drive from Santander, is the Parador Nacional 'Río Deva' at Fuente Dé, right at the heart of the most impressively precipitous part of the range.

As well as outstanding scenery, the Picos de Europa has a magnificent array of flora and fauna. You are unlikely to spot the wolves, bears and wild boar which are said to dwell still in the remoter parts of the mountains, but you will almost certainly spot eagles and vultures wheeling and circling among the mountain peaks – ibex and chamois also make frequent appearances.

It's easy to spot the tourists in this part of the world – they are the ones *not* in Land Rovers. It's not difficult to see why the preferred mode of transport is a four-wheel-drive vehicle: come the first snows of winter, anyone without one is unlikely to travel far from home. But even in high summer, many of the smaller roads in the Picos are rough going, and if you're keen to explore the most remote parts of the Picos, a Land Rover or jeep is indispensable – you can hire one in a number of the major centres such as Potes, La Hermida, Espinama or Arenas de Cabrales.

Holidaymakers' reports

'Spectacular' R Glover

'Wonderful scenery, and peaceful' Mrs J M Bendall

'Stunning' J Brooks

'Do not stay in Fuente Dé for more than three days as returning on the same road everyday from Potes gets boring!' Mr & Mrs T F Read

'Magnificent scenery; cable-car ride at Fuente Dé a must. Whole area particularly beautiful in autumn, particularly the deciduous forests' Mr Gibbs

'Don't hesitate, go before the area is ruined by tourist development' A Sexton

'Such magnificent, scenic beauty at the Embalse del Ebro as I can never forget; contrasting colours (a painter's and photographer's paradise)' D M Morris

▶ What to see

Passes and gorges The enduring memory of the Picos is of its dramatic gorges and passes. The first you will probably meet on the drive from Santander is the Desfiladero de La Hermida which you follow from Panes to Potes. It's been described as the Spanish Grand Canyon; certainly the huge, sheer sides of the ravine which dwarf the little village of La Hermida are very impressive.

West from Panes to Cangas de Onis are the less dramatic but equally impressive Cares Gorges. On the early part of the drive from Panes, take care on the twisting, turning road; it's extremely slow going – allow at least an hour and a half for the 54km drive.

The two other passes that you can drive along are the San Glorio Pass which runs 113km south-west from Potes to Oseja de Sajambre and, perhaps the best drive of all, the Sella 'defile' from Cangas de Onis southwards to Oseja de Sajambre. Both drives offer dramatic scenery and memorable views.

Potes A charming little mountain village, which offers a pleasant resting point on the drive up to Fuente Dé. Gathered around the old Infantado Tower, now restored as the town hall, Potes is placed in a remarkably beautiful spot, with the high mountain peaks as a superb backdrop.

▶ Where to stay

Parador Nacional del Río Deva, Fuente Dé £££ ☎ 942 730001
The building is undistinguished and some of the staff are graduates of Fawlty Towers, but for lovers of the mountains the setting makes up for everything. The jagged Picos tower above Fuente Dé (where you're already more than 1000 metres above sea level) to heights of some 2600 metres. A cable-car starting only yards away takes you right up into the peaks themselves.

Holidaymakers' reports

'Nice rooms, clean. Menu monotonous, no salads or vegetables – and nobody could speak English' Mr & Mrs T F Read

'Picturesque; bad points were squeaky floors and lack of noise insulation between rooms' Mr Speller

'Good food; noisy plumbing.' A Sexton

'Watch out for snow in May!' Celia Thomas

'Good service and good food' Doris and Tom Young

Alternatives The high, rustic valley of the Deva has quite a lot of neat tourist accommodation which may not enjoy the spectacular setting of the Parador at the end of the road, but which is close enough to get you to the cable-car without much delay – and which is likely to have a bit more charm. The **Del Oso** (££ ☎ 942 730418) at Cosgaya is a good bet – a smart new Alpine-style place, not too far down the valley. Further south, reached over the dramatic Puerto de Piedrasluengas and only on the fringes of the Picos, is the Parador Nacional de Fuentes Carrionas at Cervera de Pisuerga (£££ ☎ 988 870105), which is a new but beautifully constructed hotel – not as remote as Fuente Dé but in its way more secluded, with grand views of the mountains.

■ SANTANDER

'There is never any doubt, then, that one has arrived in Spain .... There is a faint sound of drums, a smell of crude olive-oil, and a current of strong, leaking electricity,' wrote Anthony Carson in 'A Train to Tarragona'. Arriving in Santander, the clues may be different but the conclusion is the same.

The previous day you were in Plymouth, pulling past the Hoe – the statue of Drake in the foreground, and beyond it the safe, gentle hills of Devon. And now you are drawing into Spain; from far away, the first impression is of the surprising green-ness of everything (not too different from Devon!) but then you begin to make out the shape of the huge mountains of the Picos de Europa: perhaps cloaked in mist, maybe covered in snow. You weren't expecting such mountains.

And then as the ferry carefully edges its way towards the port you pass by an elegant seaside resort, a wide sandy beach, something that looks like a royal palace – and is that a casino? But then the smart resort slips by and you come to the port area. Noisy and busy; huge trains clank by, cars race along blowing their horns. The buildings look shabby and unkempt – and intriguing. You are confused. Which is the real Northern Spain?

There is a natural temptation to speed away from any port of arrival – to get on with the business of exploring the country you've come to see – and here it may be stronger than usual. But Santander, more than most ports, has claims on your time. It's true that the centre of the town – just inland from the dockside – has no particular appeal for the visitor. It is mainly modern, having been reconstructed in the wake of a disastrous fire whipped up by a freak tornado in 1941. It is a comfortable, prosperous city centre and nothing more. But as you have probably guessed from your journey into port, Santander has two faces, and from the dockside you're seeing only one of them.

The other face is that smart resort you passed – El Sardinero, over the hill to the north-east of the city centre. A splendid sandy beach (also called El Sardinero) stretches between two headlands, with apartment blocks, villas and a few hotels behind the neat prom, which is laid out with flower borders and shady trees. The beach is actually split into two sections (or three if you count a small southerly extension); on the prom behind the main *primera playa* there are pavement cafés and restaurants, and behind them the big casino. It may not be Monte-Carlo or St-Tropez, but by comparison with most British seaside resorts it is stylish and attractive.

The headland to the north of the bay – Cabo Menor – is an open picnicking area; beyond it are the lighthouse and restaurant of the higher Cabo Mayor. Across the bay to the south, separating this bay from the main Bahia de Santander, is the Peninsula de la Magdalena – a public park closed to cars giving views of both aspects of Santander.

Holidaymakers' reports
'Fascinating shops' Mr Hallam

▶ What to see

Museum of prehistory and archaeology You have to be up with the lark to catch this museum open, and we confess that we never made it; that's our loss, since by all accounts there are some impressive prehistoric finds from the caves which riddle this province – decorated bones and antlers, for example.

Cathedral Not the most remarkable of cathedrals – most is of fairly recent vintage; but the Romanesque–Gothic crypt, which is used as a church, is sturdily impressive and has the unusual feature of a partially glazed floor, through which excavations of Roman and medieval remains can be glimpsed.

▶ Nearby

Santillana del Mar SW, 35km by road. This perfectly preserved medieval village shouldn't be missed by anyone who goes to Santander – or at least, anyone with a car; see separate chapter on Santillana del Mar.

Isla and Noja E, 40km by road. See Laredo.

Puente Viesgo caves SW, 30km by road. This is one of the best places in the area to see prehistoric cave paintings in the flesh, as it were – unlike those of Altamira, these are not the preserve of serious students of the prehistoric. Once out of the commercial sprawl south of Santander, an easy drive through lovely countryside brings you to the village of Puente Viesgo, and a short mountain road takes you up to the caves (and good views from the car park). You must take a guided tour, and they may go at longish intervals in low season. The paintings are mainly outlines of animals, and remarkably lifelike bearing in mind their simplicity. The El Castillo cave offers dramatic evidence of its pre-historic habitation in the numerous wall paintings – and the dramatic hand-prints on the walls.

Peña Cabarga S, 20km by road. Look more-or-less south from Santander and you'll see an isolated hill with a mast on top; that is Peña Cabarga, and with a little courage you can drive up to the top and enjoy superb views – not only of Santander (which is not the prettiest of sights from the south) but also of the mountains and coastline for miles around. There's a café/restaurant at the top. The road up (off the main N634 road, north of the hill) is reasonably well surfaced, distinctly steep in places and not very well equipped with safety barriers – but there's nothing that need deter the average motorist.

The cordillera The mountains around Ramales de la Victoria and the Asón valley (south-east of Santander) are well worth visiting, and the Picos de Europa to the south-west are spectacular. See Laredo and Picos de Europa respectively.

▶ Where to stay

Bahia £££ ☎ 942 221700 Let us be clear: choosing a hotel in Santander is a matter of horses for courses – and in plumping for the Bahia we are presuming that what you want above all else is convenience. If you want to be able to roll off the boat into your hotel room, or vice versa, look no further than the Bahia, immediately opposite the terminal; it may not look much with all its blinds down against the southerly sun, but it is in fact a polished and comfortable city hotel.
Holidaymakers' reports
'Comfortable and inexpensive' B R White
'Good food, good price, good service' Mr & Mrs Lumsden
'Very good, efficient' M Rosenberg & L Kilpatrick
'Pleasant room, pleasant food and good staff' Michael Stone

Alternatives If what you want is a bit of a treat, away from the crowds of the city or resort areas, the choice is equally clear: the Real (££££ ☎ 942 272550), a grand hotel on the hilltop looking out over the bay, is just what the doctor ordered. If you want to make the most of the beach of El Sardinero, you have a choice of three hotels, none of them ideal. In most respects your best bet is the hotel of the same name: the Sardinero (££ ☎ 942 271100) has a bit of traditional style about it, and is ideally placed for both beach and casino – but disco noise may keep you awake. The Santemar (£££ ☎ 942 272900), a little way inland from the beach area, is shiny and clean, but soulless; and the majority view of those who have stayed there is that it is poorly run. Meanwhile, back on the beach, the simpler Rhin (££ ☎ 942 274300) also has its fans, and it is certainly adequate.

Restaurants We have favourable reports from holidaymakers on several eating places in Santander. Bar del Puerto (☎ 942 213001): 'Best food, best service and ambience'; 'Excellent food' M Ayres; 'Good food' Michael Stone. Chiqui (☎ 942 272098): 'Excellent food; magnificent view – but expensive' B R White. La Concha: 'Favourite restaurant; good choice of food, good wine list, attentive service (after initial indifference) and live piano music; but cool food' F T Clayton

Important note Thefts from cars parked in the streets of Santander are common – as they are in many European cities where tourists' cars offer rich pickings. Never leave your car unattended with valuables inside, even for just a few minutes. If you're staying overnight, make sure if you can that your car is parked off the street. The Hotel Bahia, for example, has an arrangement with a private garage a few doors from the hotel. If you have to leave your car unattended, remove all valuables.

■ SANTILLANA DEL MAR

If Disneyland were ever commissioned to produce a Spanish village of seigneurial mansions, it would look like Santillana del Mar. But Santillana is no stage-set town preserved solely for the delight of tourists. Cows are driven up and down the cobbled streets by busy farmers' boys, careless of the fact that they are blocking the way of rich visitors in their Mercedes and Jaguars. Tourists' cars have been effectively banned from the main streets of Santillana (those travelling to the hotels are tolerated, but don't take too long loading and unloading bags or you will incur the wrath of the whistle-blowing policeman who rules the streets with a rod of iron).

In other parts of Europe, indeed in other parts of Spain, Santillana would have by now been hideously commercialised. At 2pm every day, folkloric dancers would be put through their motions in the main square for the benefit of the matrons of Minneapolis. So far the worst excesses of the international tourist business have been kept at bay. Of course there are souvenir shops and post-card sellers – and restaurants. But no ice-cream vans or chip vendors. Even if it is overrun with tourists in high season, Santillana remains a gem.

Holidaymakers' reports

'Possibly nicest and most unspoilt village ever visited' Mr Mallett
'Fascinating historical interest – and extremely pretty' Mr Burrows
'Peaceful' O Hallis
'Exquisite and almost unbelievable' A B Ridgway

▶ What to see

Collegiate church A handsome Romanesque church built in the 12th and 13th centuries.

▶ Nearby

Altamira caves S, 2km. The caves at Altamira apparently contain some of the most remarkable prehistoric paintings so far discovered – on a par with those in the famous caves of the Dordogne region of France. But, like Lascaux, Altamira is closed to the casual visitor: to see the paintings, you have to apply in writing, ahead of time (and presumably demonstrate a more than touristic interest in them). There is an extensive display concerning the caves, the paintings and the civilisation they represent, housed in modern galleries; and you can visit a small cave with the usual formations of stalactites and stalagmites. No entrance charges.

Puente Viesgo caves SE, 20km by road. See Santander.

▶ Where to stay

Parador Nacional Gil Blas £££ ☎ 942 818000 Situated in the picturesque main square, this fine Parador is named after the fictional hero of the novel written by 18th-century French author Lesage. This is without doubt one of the finest Paradores in Spain; the rooms are attractively furnished, the staff are generally friendly

Parador Nacional Gil Blas

and efficient – and the food is reasonably good. Its proximity to Santander, about an hour's drive away, would have ensured its popularity even if it hadn't been such a magnficent building situated in a beauty spot. Advance booking is essential during the main season to ensure a room; even if you're only planning to stop for lunch en route to Santander, it's a good idea to reserve a table as the dining room is occasionally deluged with visiting coach parties.

Holidaymakers' reports

'Beautiful building and furnishings' Mr Mallett

'Excellent Parador; food and wine a bit expensive but good nevertheless' David & Joan Morgan

Alternatives Hotel Los Infantes (££ ☎ 942 818100) is set in a fine house, and a more than acceptable substitute for the Parador – though its position beside the road skirting the village is not ideal. 'Friendly service, comfortable' Jean Boxall, Doreen Gascoigne; 'Room good, service courteous' Mr Burrows. We also have favourable reports on the Hotel Altamira (£ ☎ 942 818025): 'Spacious rooms, medieval setting, lovely historic setting' C G Rowe

Restaurants We have two favourable reports from holidaymakers on Meson de los Blasones (☎ 942 818070): 'Our favourite restaurant; very good food, different menu to other restaurants. Could watch cooking' J & L A Bamber; 'Excellent food' W L Whiting

■ SAN VICENTE DE LA BARQUERA

San Vicente de la Barquera is a stylish little resort and long-established fishing port at the mouth of its own *ría*. There is no beach in the resort but a small sandy one within the bay to the east and a fine big sandy one on the other, Atlantic side of the easterly headland.

► Nearby

Comillas E, 10km by road. For a change of scene: a neat little resort with a small harbour west of the good beach, which is partly backed by dunes and partly by modern apartment blocks. There's a big car park and cafés immediately behind the beach, too.

► Where to stay

Miramar £ ☎ 942 710075 This neat modern hotel sits on a low headland to the west of the bay which forms the mouth of the Ría San Vicente, in charming rustic surroundings; but it's within walking distance of the old village and port in case the peace and the view from the garden begin to pall.
Holidaymakers' reports
'Good food, accommodating service' Mr & Mrs Matthews

The East

Picturesque fishing villages and smart resorts on the coast, with some dramatic scenery; ancient churches along the pilgrim routes crossing the dusty plains to the south of the *cordillera*; abundant vineyards in La Rioja.

■ BASES IN THE EAST

We have divided Northern Spain into three: the West, the Centre and the East. In each area we have sifted out those villages, towns or cities which you will probably want to use as a base – because there are interesting sights or good hotels to be found there.

Each base is the subject of a separate short chapter which provides a brief account of the place as a whole, followed by details of the sights you should see, the attractions that can be found in places nearby, the hotel or hotels where you should stay – and alternative accommodation you might consider if rooms don't happen to be available in our selected hotels. We have also included, where appropriate, comments from holidaymakers who have completed questionnaires distributed by Brittany Ferries and from readers who have taken the first edition of the guide with them on holiday in Northern Spain.

These are our bases in the East:

Hotel prices are indicated by ratings. In 1987, prices for a double room with bath are roughly as follows:

£	under £20
££	£20 to £30
£££	£30 to £40
££££	£40 to £55
£££££	£55 to £75

■ INTRODUCTION

It has to be admitted that the high-spots of Northern Spain (literal or figurative) are to be found not here but further west – the mountains cannot match the drama or the altitude of the Picos de Europa, the churches are outshone by the magnificent cathedrals of Burgos, León and Santiago, even the hotels do not achieve the exceptional standards reached by a handful further west. But in the east there is an astonishing variety of terrain and tourist interest – from glorious coastal scenery and glossy beach resorts such as San Sebastián to parched cereal-growing plains inland, where the communities range from the simplest village to thriving modern cities; if the spice of life is what you are after, this area perhaps offers more of it than the west or the centre.

Much though not all of the area is Basque country, where a language and culture quite distinct from those of Spain flourish. It's easy to exaggerate how much this will mean to the casual visitor; everyone notices the curiously spelt place-names, which often have an X or a K or a Z where you would least expect it – and you can't fail to notice the insistent use of spray paint to obliterate those road signs which use the Spanish spellings rather than the Basque ones. But in most respects you're unlikely to be aware of when you're in Basque territory and when you're not. There are political tensions in the region, because some people would like to see the Basque country separated from Spain – and this is occasionally made manifest in outbreaks of violence. The risk has never seemed high enough to affect our travel plans in the area – most of the violence, when it occurs, is fairly precisely aimed at Spanish officials; but it is clearly prudent to keep an eye on the news in the run-up to your trip, in case the temperature is raised.

The area we cover in this section corresponds more-or-less to that of the three provinces of Pais Vasco/Euskadi, Navarra and La Rioja. We have not gone into the furthest southern corners of Navarra and La Rioja, but we have strayed a little way into Castilla-León in the west, and into Aragon in the south-east. Our 'bases' include big, booming cities and out-of-the-way towns and villages.

Costa Verde
SANTANDER
Llanes
San Vicente de la Barquera
Comillas
Santillana del Mar
Suances
Isla
Noja
Laredo
Castro Urdiales
Plencia
Cuevas de Altamira
Torrelavega
N634
Puente Viesgo
Desfiladero de la Hermida
Potes
CANTABRIA
N611
N623
BILBAO
Río Nervión
Puerto de Piedrasluengas
Puerto de San Glorio
Alto Campóo
Embalse del Ebro
Puerto del Escudo
Reinosa
Orduña
Puerto de Orduña
Cervera de Pisuerga
Río Ebro
Aguilar de Campóo
N625
LEON
Oña
Frías
Embalse de Sobrón
Herrera de Pisuerga
N623
Pancorbo
Miranda de Ebro
MONTES DE OCA
N1
A1
Villadiego
Briviesca
Osorno
N120
Villanueva de Argaño
N611
Villoldo
Frómista
BURGOS
Río Oja
N620
SIERRA DE LA DEMAN
N1
Monzón de Campos
PALENCIA

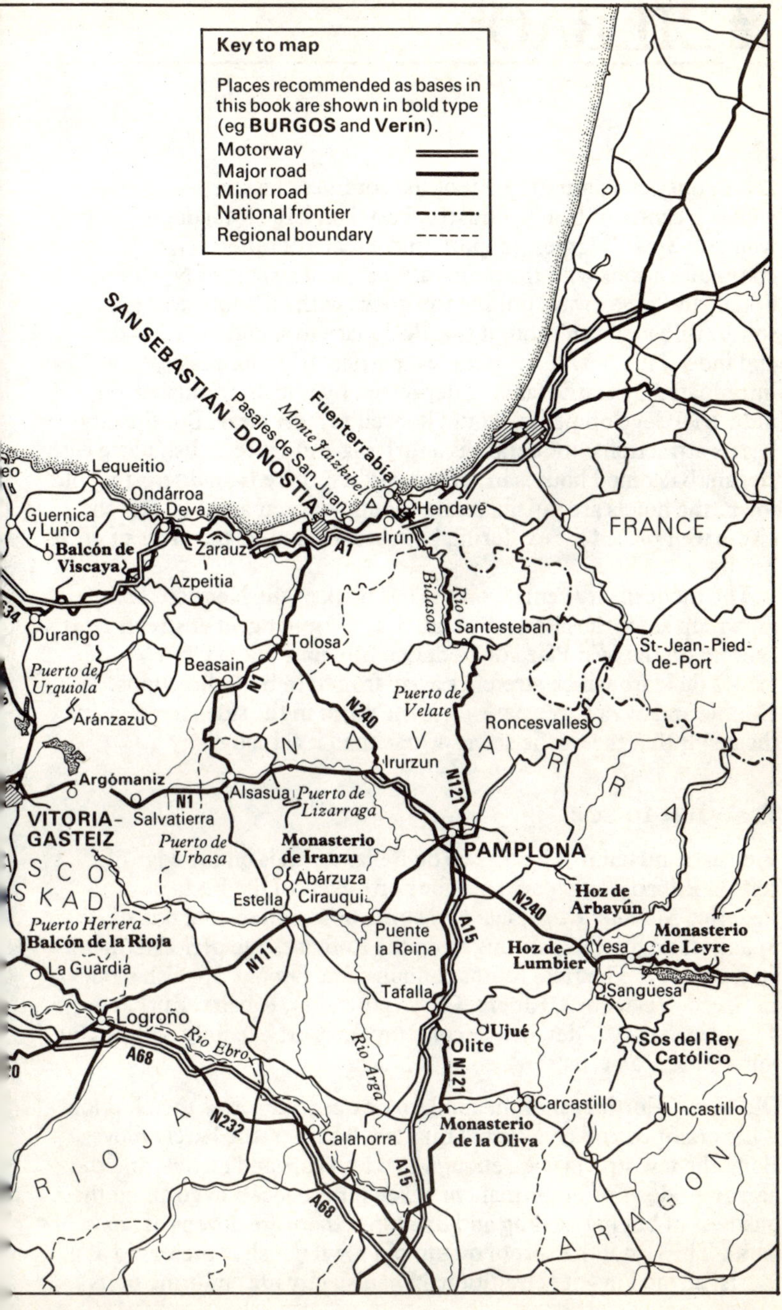

Key to map
Places recommended as bases in this book are shown in bold type (eg **BURGOS** and **Verín**).
Motorway
Major road
Minor road
National frontier
Regional boundary
SAN SEBASTIÁN-DONOSTIA
Pasajes de San Juan
Monte Jaizkibel
Fuenterrabia
Hendaye
Irún
FRANCE
Lequeitio
Ondárroa
Deva
Guernica y Luno
Balcón de Viscaya
Zarauz
A1
Azpeitia
Río Bidasoa
Santesteban
St-Jean-Pied-de-Port
Durango
Tolosa
Beasain
N1
Puerto de Urquiola
N240
Puerto de Velate
Aránzazu
Roncesvalles
N A V A R R A
Irurzun
Argómaniz
Alsasua
Puerto de Lizarraga
N121
Salvatierra
VITORIA-GASTEIZ
Puerto de Urbasa
Monasterio de Iranzu
PAMPLONA
Abárzuza
Cirauqui
Estella
Hoz de Arbayún
N240
Puerto Herrera
Balcón de la Rioja
Puente la Reina
A15
Monasterio de Leyre
Yesa
Hoz de Lumbier
N111
La Guardia
Sangüesa
Tafalla
Logroño
Río Ebro
Ujué
Olite
Sos del Rey Católico
A68
Río Arga
N121
Carcastillo
Uncastillo
N232
Calahorra
Monasterio de la Oliva
A15
A68
R I O J A
A R A G O N

■ BILBAO

A big, busy city, bursting out of the confines of a steep-sided river valley; a centre of heavy industry, based on large local deposits of iron ore; Spain's largest seaport, and a focus of other communications with the main international airport of Northern Spain, and motorways linking the docks with all points east and south; Bilbao doesn't sound the ideal place to spend your holiday, and indeed it's not. Many people – particularly those easily intimidated by traffic jams or depressed by uncompromising industrial development – would do well to steer clear. But the city has its attractions: the centre is a thriving and quite stylish place with elegant balconied houses in some quarters, there is an interesting old town, the hotels are satisfactory although not remarkable, and the city is well placed for exploring both coastal and inland areas of great beauty.

The modern city centre, on the left bank of the Nervion, has grown up since the late 19th century as a regular grid of streets centred on the oval Plaza de Federico Moyúa and the Gran Via de López de Haro which stretches away from it in both directions. Double and even triple parking is the norm in the side streets, with the result that the traffic seems worse than it actually is.

▶ What to see

Fine arts museum The Museo de Bellas Artes is on the edge of central Bilbao's only park, not far north-west of the Plaza de Federico Moyúa. The old gallery contains an interesting mix of Spanish and foreign painting from the Romanesque period to the 20th century. The final rooms contain some famous Spanish names – El Greco, Velázquez, Ribera, Goya (portraits), Ribalta, Zurbarán. The new gallery is devoted to contemporary art – mainly Spanish but some American artists.

Old town North-east of the modern city centre, across the Nervion, is the cramped and chaotic old quarter, where traffic barely moves along the few streets wide enough to admit cars and lorries, and the narrower alleys offer permanent shade for the locals to go about their business of buying, selling and drinking (there are dozens of *tapas* bars). This is not the sort of quaint old town which is preserved as a tourist attraction – it is traditional Spanish city life enduring of its own accord, largely unaffected by the modern pace and style of the rest of the city.

Monte Archanda To the north of Bilbao a minor road winding along the flank of Monte Archanda gives stupendous views over the city, the river and the docks. It can hardly be called a pretty sight, but it is certainly impressive – rarely can you see a major city from such a vantage point.

▶ Nearby

The coast from Bilbao to Deva This entire stretch of coast is high, often verging on the mountainous, with just the occasional interruption where a valley breaches the cliffs. In each of these breaches, a fishing village has grown up; some have become big fishing villages, others small resorts, others something between the two. With the exception of Zarauz, at the extreme eastern end (and only a few miles from San Sebastián), none deserves to be thought of as a place to stay – though they're not devoid of accommodation if a night or two off the main tourist track appeals to you. Bilbao and San Sebastián are linked by motorway, which means that you can easily make a complete round-trip from one end or the other – you'd need only an hour to get back to base.

Algorta, an affluent residential satellite of Bilbao at the mouth of the heavily industrialised river Nervion, forms the western extremity of this scenic coast. (It has an attractive-sounding hotel, Los Tamarises, which we were quite unable to find!) The coast road takes you at first past a succession of sandy beaches before going inland through hilly countryside. At Plencia, a river leads into an enclosed bay with a long sandy beach, very popular with Bilbaoans. After another attractive inland stretch, you meet the coast again at tiny Arminza; the next 25km or so is a succession of magnificent coastal views, spoilt only by a nuclear power station crammed into one of the valleys (you're warned as you enter the area that there's no stopping for 5km). There are parking areas and seats at the major viewpoints. Just east of Baquio, one such viewpoint looks down on the church of San Juan de Gaztelugache, built on an outcrop of rock out in the sea and linked by a causeway looking like a miniature Wall of China.

Bermeo is a thriving fishing port near the mouth of a substantial inlet; at its inland end stands Guernica, a small town which would be unremarkable were it not the spiritual capital of the Basque country. During the Civil War, it paid a high price for its stature: the town was flattened by German bombing, an infamous act of savagery captured in Picasso's famous painting – for many years kept in New

York but now on view in the Casón del Buen Retiro in Madrid.

From Guernica you have a choice of routes eastward – back up the *ría* to carry on following the coast, or an inland short-cut to Lequeitio. The fact that the latter isn't accorded 'scenic' status by the tourist maps needn't put you off: the road goes through charming hilly countryside.

Lequeitio is the undoubted star of this coast: its harbour is lined by tall, narrow, slightly ramshackle houses with balconies clothed in many-paned windows and backed by an elevated square where the population gathers in the evening to talk or roller-skate, depending on age. Immediately behind this is the church of Santa Maria,

The harbour at Lequeitio

rebuilt at the end of the 15th century and worth investigating if you find it unlocked. The harbour itself, like every other on this coast, is crammed with colourfully painted fishing boats large and (mainly) small. Just east of the harbour wall is a good sandy beach, and there's another further along beyond the mouth of the little river, facing the offshore islet of San Nicolás.

Ondárroa doesn't have such an interesting harbour, but does enjoy a charming setting at the mouth of its river; the church is perched high on arcades beside the river, which is crossed by a fine stone foot-bridge as well as the road-bridge. There is a good beach not far away at Saturraran.

The Nervion valley S, 40km or so by road. This grand canyon, as it were, is within easy reach of Bilbao – by motorway if you prefer. See Vitoria.

▶ Where to stay

Hotel Carlton £££ ☎ 944 162200 The Carlton is no longer considered the best hotel in town by those who care about mod cons, but it still enjoys the best position – right on the Plaza Federico Moyúa – and for our money is still the most appealing. It is traditional in style, and no doubt has seen better days, but it still has an elegant lobby and lounge, and spacious bedrooms. Don't be tempted to dine here – the dining room is entirely without atmosphere, the service and food barely tolerable; fortunately the city has plenty of highly reputed restaurants at all price levels.

Alternatives There are several other decent city-centre hotels, all modern and all lacking the airiness of the Carlton – their public rooms generally admit little or no natural light. The five-star Villa de Bilbao (£££££ ☎ 944 416000) is currently regarded as best in town; lots of chrome, glass and leather, and plenty of space in the public rooms – but the gloss is already beginning to wear off. The Aránzazu (£££ ☎ 944 413100) has an attractive bar area, but a distinctly tatty dining room. The Grand Hotel Ercilla (££££ ☎ 944 438800) is very business-oriented; its near-subterranean public rooms are spacious and well maintained but a bit gloomy.

FUENTERRABÍA

This historic fortified town stands just to the west of the mouth of the Río Bidasoa, which at this point forms the frontier between Spain and France. Fortunately, both road and railway miss the town by a mile or two, and it is Irún to the south which has suffered the usual border-town blight; Fuenterrabía remains, enclosed within its walls, a charming haven. Its particular attraction is that the centrepiece, the Palace of Carlos V, is now a Parador – and comes as close as a hotel could to giving you the feeling that you really are living in a part of the past (see 'Where to stay'). The town around the hill-top palace is calm and picturesque, with balconied old houses lining the narrow streets.

▶ What to see

Palace of Carlos V You can't miss this severe edifice in the main square – though it would be easy to miss the fact that it is a hotel. Most of the palace is reserved for guests, but casual visitors can take a drink in the gallery bar at one end of the magnificent entrance hall. The palace dates from the 11th century, but most of the existing building is of 14th-, 15th- or 16th-century origin.

Calle Mayor Leading from the decorated Puerta de Santa Maria (the main gateway through the encircling walls) to the palace, this main street has a particularly fine collection of old houses, and takes you past the Ayuntamiento and the church of Nuestra Señora de la Asunción – originally Gothic, but later remodelled in Renaissance style.

▶ Nearby

Monte Jaizkibel W, 10km or so by road. Fuenterrabía is separated from Pasajes de San Juan (see San Sebastián) by this high, bare mountain. A good road traverses the length of it, giving fine views to seaward for most of the way and to landward at either end.

Valle del Bidasoa SE, 40km or so by road. Fuenterrabía lies on the west side of the mouth of the Bidasoa; on the east side is French Hendaye, gateway to the delights of the French resorts of St-Jean-de-Luz and Biarritz. The border goes off roughly south-eastwards, following the Pyrenees, while the valley of the Bidasoa winds away in a more southerly direction towards Pamplona. It's a charming, green valley with an increasingly Alpine atmosphere as you climb gently towards Santesteban. The fields are dotted with big old houses with shallow-pitched roofs and wooden balconies under overhanging eaves, and in the villages along the way the houses are decorated with plaques and potted plants. Beyond Santesteban you start to climb more steeply towards the fine mountainous scenery of the Puerto de Velate (847m); soon after the col, the countryside begins to take on something of the parched look of central Spain, as meadows give way to cereal fields and the forests thin out.

▶ Where to stay

Parador Nacional El Emperador £££ ☎ 943 642140 One of the grandest of Paradores, occupying the central keep of the fortress town. It's difficult to imagine a more striking hotel lobby than the cool, dark vault into which you step from the heat of the central square. The first impression is maintained – although of course modern amenities have been installed, you still get the feeling that you are staying in a medieval castle.

Alternatives There are other hotels in Fuenterrabía – the best of them the Jáuregui (££ ☎ 943 641400) – and rooms to let in neat-looking houses in the old town. But a visit rather loses its point if you're not staying at the Parador; book early.

■OLITE

A small town in the centre of an extensive plain stands at a natural disadvantage compared with hill-top competitors. But Olite has got what it takes to overcome such handicaps – principally a palace-cum-castle which would do credit to any fairy tale; approach Olite (as the postcards do) from the east, and you'll be drawn irresistibly by the romantic vision of the high crenellated towers of the castle, dominating the town. In practice, you're more likely to be following the signs to the Parador from the main road between Pamplona in the north and Soria and Zaragoza in the south. But the result is the same: part of the delight of Olite is that its chief attraction and its only substantial hotel are one and the same – the Parador *is* the castle of the kings of Navarra.

Olite is a prosperous little country town, its narrow streets accommodating one or two neat bars and restaurants as well as a few shops and lots of flower-bedecked balconies. It makes a pleasant stroll before dinner – and there's no danger of getting lost, with the towers of the castle to guide you back to base.

► What to see

The castle The castle-cum-palace was given its present form in the 15th century, when Carlos III moved his court here; if the round towers strike you as French rather than Spanish in style, go to the top of the class – Carlos himself had French connections, and employed French architects in the construction. The turrets and fortifications are reminiscent of the Palace of the Popes at Avignon, though it is on nothing like the same scale. The Parador occupies a small part of the building, but the greater part is open to the public (small entrance fee) via a separate door beyond the church of Santa Maria. Steep stone stairs take you up to the battlements, which purists will find over-neatly restored, but which most visitors will find a joy. So complete and so complex is the arrangement of walls and towers that you can get lost wandering around them; and because the structure is so irregular each bit of the battlements opens up new views of other bits – as well as the town spread out below and the fertile plain stretching away to the brown hills of Aragon to the east.

Churches Literally next door to the Parador is the beautifully sculptured doorway of the little Gothic church of Santa Maria, once the palace chapel; there is apparently more decoration inside, but you are unlikely to find the door open. If you've been on to the walls of the castle you'll have had a good view of San Pedro a little way to the south. Of Romanesque origin, much of it is 12th- and 13th-century Gothic; its tower is topped by a soaring spire, and the main doorway is highly ornate – it includes two eagles symbolising violence and gentleness.

▶ Nearby

Monasterio de La Oliva SW, 35km by road. Amid flat fertile countryside on the left bank of the Aragon, the church of La Oliva has the distinction of being the oldest Gothic edifice in Spain. It is a fairly plain affair, apart from some unusual Greek-style decoration on the main front and decorated capitals to the main pillars inside.

The rib vaulting is crude and massive. It is a sizeable church, dark and dank with windows which are either small or relatively non-transparent, being made of marble rather than glass. The adjacent 15th-century Gothic cloisters make a pleasant airy contrast. Don't miss the simple, elegantly vaulted chapterhouse.

Estella NW, 40km by road. See Pamplona.

Ujué NE, 20km by road. Time almost seems to have passed by this hilltop village, which has an unusual fortified church dating from the 11th century; splendid views towards the broad valley of the Ebro, to the south.

Sierra de Leyre NE, 70km or so by road. See Sos del Rey Católico.

Tafalla N, 5km by road. The church of Santa Maria contains a notable Renaissance altarpiece.

▶ Where to stay

Parador Nacional Principe de Viana £££ ☎ 948 740000 The shell of a part of the Palace has been successfully converted into the core of the hotel – a grand lounge (with huge stone fireplace, apparently put to good use in winter) and dining room on the ground floor and a handful of bedrooms, some of them extravagantly spacious, above. Antique ornaments abound, but on the other hand some of the other furnishings are beginning to look a bit antique. A substantial new extension houses a bar which by Parador standards is cosy, plus the majority of the bedrooms – not quite as grand as those in the old part, but still very comfortable. Service and meals conform to the normal Parador standards – that is, unremarkable.

Alternatives Olite isn't the sort of place you should miss just because you can't get a room at the Parador. A modern, functional but competent alternative is the Tafalla (£ ☎ 948 700300), 4km north beside the Pamplona road.

PAMPLONA

'The fiesta was really started. It kept up day and night for seven days. The dancing kept up, the drinking kept up, the noise went on. The things that happened could only have happened during a fiesta. Everything became quite unreal finally and it seemed as though nothing could have any consequences. It seemed out of place to think of consequences during the fiesta. All during the fiesta you had the feeling even when it was quiet, that you had to shout any remark to make it heard. It was the same feeling about any action. It was a fiesta and it went on for seven days.

'... When I woke it was the sound of the rocket exploding that announced the release of the bulls from the corrals at the edge of town. They would race through the streets and out to the bull-ring ... Down below the narrow street was empty. All the balconies were crowded with people. Suddenly a crowd came down the street. They were all running, packed close together. They passed along and up the street towards the bull ring and behind them came more men running faster, and then some stragglers who were really running. Behind them was a little bare space, and then the bulls galloping, tossing their heads up and down. It all went out of sight around the corner. One man fell, rolled to the gutter, and lay quiet. But the bulls went right on and did not notice him. They were all running together.'

Ernest Hemingway's novel *Fiesta* (or *The Sun also Rises*) not only captured splendidly the atmosphere of Pamplona's Fiesta de San Fermín – it has also played no small part in making it more widely known than any other of Spain's fiestas. The result is that the city attracts huge numbers of visitors during the fiesta (in early July), eager to see the bulls to be slaughtered each evening being run into the city centre along the streets, instead of being delivered directly to the bull ring in the normal way; anyone who fancies himself (or herself) as a *torero* can run ahead of the bulls (and take the consequences). During the fiesta (when there are parades, fireworks and other events too), hotel rates zoom to ludicrous heights, and even so you have to book well ahead to get a room. At other times of the year, Pamplona offers little of particular interest to the tourist, but it is an agreeable place nonetheless, with some decent restaurants in and around the old quarter, north of the centre, and glossy shops in the spacious areas south of the centre. It is also a good base for excursions in all directions – Olite and the countryside north of Sos del Rey Católico would be well within range.

▶ What to see

Cathedral Tucked away among narrow streets in the north-east corner of the old town, the cathedral is not an immediately impressive edifice. The classical west façade (added in the 18th century) is gaudily amusing and the original Gothic wooden doors of the north porch are still there to be seen, but most of the interest lies inside – and it is quite likely to be locked. There are several small chapels around the apse and along the sides, with notable works of art dating from the 14th, 15th and 16th centuries; in the Capilla Mayor are fine carved stalls. In the nave is the beautifully carved alabaster tomb of King Carlos III and his wife Leonor of Castile. The Gothic cloisters, reached from the south transept, are unusually gracious and grand, with interesting doorways and other carvings. From the north door of the cathedral it is only a few yards to the old walls of the city, with views of the new Pamplona rising up across the river Arga, and of the low hills beyond to the north; following the walls anticlockwise brings you to the museum.

Museo de Navarra From what we read this sounds a more than averagely interesting provincial museum, with archaeological finds (Roman mosaics), an ethnological collection, Romanesque details saved from the original cathedral building and paintings ranging from the Romanesque period to the 18th century. Sadly it was closed for renovation when we were there.

Ayuntamiento The town hall façade may be architecturally undistinguished but it has been painted up a treat.

▶ Nearby

Sierra de Andia and Sierra de Urbasa This day-trip to the west of the city could also be undertaken from Vitoria or other bases. Depending on how you time the trip, it may be a good idea to take a picnic – though there are decent restaurants en route at Alsasua, Estella and Puente La Reina. There is definitely a right way round to do this tour, which is the way we describe it here.

The exit from Pamplona is on a minor road going more-or-less due west from the city, off the main San Sebastián road. With luck, you soon emerge on to the rolling wheatfields which line the river Arga; and as the river starts to turn south towards its eventual meeting with the Aragon and Ebro, you start to climb the forested flank of the Sierra de Sarvil. The road climbs steadily, opening up immense views ranging from Pamplona and the Pyrenees in the east to Puente la Reina in the south. In summer and autumn, the green of the tall trees lining the river (and of the occasional irrigated field) stands out in a parched expanse of brown and gold. Just before the col at 840m – about 450m (1500ft) above the river – is a viewing platform. From here for about 15km the road winds gently downwards through hilly wheatfields dotted with small settlements to Abárzuza, where you leave the Estella road.

Your main route turns northward here, but there is a worthwhile short diversion to the Monasterio de Iranzu. The monastery is about 2km up a peaceful gorge; it dates from the 12th century, but has now been restored and re-occupied. From Abárzuza you climb into the high, dry limestone country of the Sierra de Andia; pause occasionally to take in the extensive views back over the Embalse de Alloz (a man-made lake) miles to the south-east. Eventually, the road disappears into a tunnel, as if to reinforce the drama of what awaits you on the other side of the *sierra*; it barely needs reinforcement – a tremendous view across a steep-sided valley to the peak of Beriain and down on to the village of Lizarraga. A couple of hundred yards down from the tunnel is a viewpoint, and the road then winds down the precipitous mountainside.

The broad valley of the Araquil has felt the impact of huge industrial development, but at Alsasua you turn south out of it, on a small hairpin road which delivers you eventually on to the high Sierra de Urbasa – a rocky, forested table-land where fine sturdy horses roam, bells on their necks like the cattle of the Alps. It's a pleasant area for a picnic or a snooze under a tree, but the spectaular bit comes (again) just after you reach the high-point of the *sierra* (920m) near its southern extremity – glorious views down into the lush valleys leading to Estella, and the neat village of Baquedano on the opposing hillside. Behind you as you descend the steep slope are massive rocky outcrops. After a few miles of pleasant although unspectacular countryside you arrive at Estella.

Estella and Puente La Reina Estella is less than an hour from Pamplona along the main N111 road, making it possible to visit this old town and several other points of interest along the way in a long half-day-trip. This section takes things in an easterly order, to suit those who have arrived at Estella via the *sierras* (see above).

Estella is of Roman origin, and has played important roles throughout history – not least because it lies on one of the main pilgrim routes to Santiago. It has countless palaces and churches – outstanding among them San Pedro de la Rúa, dating from the 12th century. Perched on a steep slope across the river from the modern town, its imposing tower looks more military than ecclesiastical; steps lead up to the splendidly decorated doorway, which shows clear Moorish influence in its multiple lobes. On the other side of the church are the charming remains of the simple Romanesque cloister;

if you can't get through the church to it, you can at least get a look at it by descending the steps and taking the next alley along the street. Close by in this same quarter of the town are the fine Renaissance Ayuntamiento, with coats of arms on the façade, and a rare example of non-religious Romanesque architecture in the Palacio de los Duques de Granada de Ega.

Just off the Estella–Puenta road, a few miles east of Estella, is the charming hill-top village of Cirauqui; it has not yet been spoilt by tourists and makes no concessions to them – if you want to get up to see the notable doorway of the church of San Román (like that of San Pedro de la Rúa in Estella, polylobed in the Moorish manner), you either toil up the rough streets on foot or pick your way round the back streets and farmyards. A few more miles' driving brings you to Puente la Reina, where the two main pilgrims' routes from the Pyrenees to Santiago converged to cross the Río Arga: the elegant bridge built for their convenience in the 11th century is still there today. There are several churches in the town worth seeing.

Not far away on the road east of Puente la Reina (not the road for Pamplona) is another striking remnant of the pilgrims' days – the church of Santa Maria at Eunate. An octagonal church is in itself a considerable curiosity; such a church in the middle of fields, miles from the nearest community of any size, seems positively bizarre. The theory is that the church served as a place of burial for pilgrims who fell on their journey to Santiago.

▶ Where to stay

There is no single hotel which makes an obvious recommendation for Pamplona. Supposedly the best in town, with five stars to its name, is Los Tres Reyes (£££££ ☎ 948 226600); it's spacious, has a quite attractive outdoor pool, garage space and air conditioning, and is quite conveniently set on a busy through road on the west side of the centre; but it is no longer new, and is entirely without atmosphere or genuine style – and much more expensive than the alternatives. In the midst of the old town (and not so convenient for motorists), the Maisonnave (££ ☎ 948 222600) is a satisfactory middle-of-the-road hotel, newish but striving for a bit of traditional style. The Orhi (££ ☎ 948 245800), close to the bull ring on the fringe of the southern, modern part of the centre, is a well-run alternative. The Yoldi (£ ☎ 948 224800) is slightly cheaper and simpler, in a slightly more central street. The shiny new Ciudad de Pamplona (££ ☎ 948 266011) is curiously set in an equally new but rather less shiny residential suburb, south-west of the city.

SAN SEBASTIÁN

The ideal way to to arrive in San Sebastián would be by private plane, at twilight, approaching the airport from the west. Look out of the right-hand window as you lose height, and you'd see in all its glory the reason why San Sebastián has grown up to be the major resort on the north coast of Spain, and an impressive seaside resort by any standard. The blazing reflections of the lights along its prom stretch around a complete semi-circle, and more; at either end are headlands – to the west, rising to near-mountainous heights, Monte Igueldo is topped by the lights of one of the resorts's best hotels; to the east, the lower peak of Monte Urgull serves as the base of a huge illuminated statue of Christ.

If you arrive by more down-to-earth means, it is still best to approach from the west – to the east of the resort are grimy dockland and industrial areas which will not whet your appetite. And for a good approximation to the view from mid-air you can drive up to the top of Monte Igueldo before going in to the town. You could do a lot worse than to stay atop Monte Igueldo for the night, and hope for a spectacular sunrise over the Pyrenees. What you'll miss by doing so (unless you have the patience to make the fifteen-minute journey down the hill and round the bay) is the atmosphere and facilities of downtown San Sebastián, which is that rarest of things – a smart, interesting, lively, prosperous, cosmopolitan seaside resort.

What you won't see on your arrival in the gloaming is the splendid sandy beach which runs around the bay – or, strictly, the beaches: the main beach of La Concha, backed by a prom about a mile and a half in length, is separated from the smaller Ondarreta by a low headland, where the seafront road is forced briefly to resort to tunnelling. Offshore at the mouth of the bay, fending off the vigour of the Atlantic, is the substantial islet of Santa Clara – reachable by boat during the day and floodlit at night to add to the drama of the scene.

The main part of the town is at the east end of the bay, either side of the broad Río Urumea. Most of it is fairly modern – the resort became fashionable in the late 19th century, when the Royal Family began to spend its summers here; it is spacious and quite elegant, with tree-lined avenues and a sprinkling of grand buildings – the Ayuntamiento (originally the casino) close to the beach, the Palacio de la Diputación and the 19th-century neo-Gothic Cathedral of the Good Shepherd. Even the old town behind the small harbour (see below) is not actually very old, having been largely rebuilt after the devastating fires of the Peninsular War in 1813. A pleasant prom dotted with trees runs along high above La Concha beach, and there are several areas of garden elsewhere in the town.

▶ What to see

Old town Despite its lack of antiquity, the old town presents a sharp contrast to the broad boulevards of the rest of the resort. Squeezed on to the peninsula at the foot of Monte Urgull, between the bay and the river, its narrow streets are lined with flowered balconies, shops, bars and restaurants (including several very good ones); in season it is always animated, but activity reaches its peak in the evening, when the *tapas* bars (complete with sawdust on the floor) come to life. In the centre is the open Plaza de la Constitución, with high arcades on the fronts of its grander houses. On the northern fringe are the churches of Santa Maria (18th-century, with a strikingly elaborate façade) and San Vicente (16th-century Gothic).

Museo de San Telmo The former convent of San Telmo, dating from the 16th century, now houses the Provincial Museum, with

The view from Monte Igueldo

picture galleries as well as historical, ethnographical and archaeological displays. The building itself is also of interest, with a graceful Renaissance cloister.

Monte Urgull There are various paths up the substantial hill behind the harbour. The main reward is good views of the bay, though there is also a small military museum housed in the Castillo de Santa Cruz de la Mota. A wide promenade (Paseo Nuevo) circles the base of the hill, and where it meets the harbour there is an aquarium.

Monte Igueldo The higher peak at the far western end of the bay is worth the trip for the views it affords; children may be persuaded by the small fun-fair, with its tiny train, boating pool and dodgems. See also 'Where to stay'.

▶ Nearby

Pasajes de San Juan A couple of miles to the east of San Sebastián is a splendid natural harbour, all but enclosed by steep hills, which must at one time have been outstandingly beautiful. Today it is in general outstandingly vile, having been taken over by docks and factories; but at the mouth of the harbour are two tiny communities

which remain largely unaffected by the squalour just inland. The gem is Pasajes de San Juan, on the east of the narrows, which is best approached by ferry boat from opposing Pasajes de San Pedro; what confronts you is basically a single line of houses, some of stone, some of brightly painted wood, many decked with flowers. Once ashore, a narrow cobbled street takes you the length of the village, running underneath arches which carry the houses over it. There are several attractive fish restaurants – not surprisingly, the village is a popular place for a meal out with a difference.

Monte Jaizkibel See Fuenterrabía.

▶ Where to stay

Monte Igueldo ££££ ☎ 943 210211 In any other position, the modern Hotel Monte Igueldo would be unremarkable; its bedrooms are satisfactory but nothing more, its public rooms spacious but devoid of atmosphere, service unreliable (see below). But it isn't in any other position, it's right on top of Monte Igueldo – and it gives spectacular views (from some rooms at least) over the beautiful Bahia de la Concha. On the roof is a mid-sized L-shaped swimming pool and a separate children's pool; the surroundings are pretty basic, the views superb, the wind sometimes too strong for comfort. If you want to sample the nightlife of San Sebastián or to make much use of its beaches the drive from Monte Igueldo – quite a way down, then a couple of miles around the bay – will be a real drawback, and you'd be better off staying in the resort itself. A funicular railway runs down the hill to the bay in the daytime.

Holidaymakers' reports

'View spectacular, service dismissive, food basic' B Norris and J Clarke

'Dining room service a shambles' Anon

Alternatives Pride of place in the resort goes to the Hotel de Londres y de Inglaterra (££££ ☎ 943 426989), right on the prom towards the eastern end of the beach – a traditional hotel with mainly elegant decor and furnishings. Not far away, just back from the prom, is the Orly (£££ ☎ 943 463200), a tall modern tower, adequately comfortable but now beginning to look a bit the worse for wear; there is a cafeteria but no restaurant. In some ways the best hotel in town is the Costa Vasca (£££ ☎ 943 211011), which from its appearance and position you could mistake for an apartment building – it is a brick-clad balconied block a good way up the hill behind the beach, in a residential area well away from the resort itself. It is stylish and spacious, and has all mod cons – including a tennis court and big pool.

■ SANTO DOMINGO DE LA CALZADA

The considerable volume of traffic between the cities of Logroño and Burgos is these days carried by major roads and motorways which take a northerly sweep via Miranda, the cross-roads of this whole area. The pilgrims of old, on their way to Santiago, took a more direct route clinging to the foothills of the Sierra de la Demanda, but it is now little more than a by-way. The residents of Santo Domingo, the major staging post on the road (where it crosses the Río Oja), may or may not be grateful to have been left aside while the concrete factories and canning plants have gone up elsewhere; but certainly the visitor should give thanks. The major environmental hazard as you sip your aperitif in the Parador in the historic centre is the shrieks of boisterous schoolchildren dispersing after classes.

▶ What to see

Cathedral The Romanesque/Gothic cathedral dominates the old part of the town north of the main road, its south door opening on to a small paved square shared with a detached Baroque belfry, the ancient chapel of Nuestra Señora de la Plaza and the Parador. Santo Domingo himself was buried here in the 12th century, but his remarkable two-storey alabaster shrine in the south transept dates from the 16th. Close by is an even greater curiosity – a live rooster and hen kept in a chamber in the west wall of the transept. They are killed and replaced each year in remembrance of an earlier cock which proved the innocence of a pilgrim by crowing from its roasting tin. The building itself is not without interest, from the finely moulded west doorway to the Plateresque high altar screen.

Hospice of Santo Domingo Otherwise known as the Parador; despite its plain-looking modern exterior, the hotel is worth a look if you are not staying – beyond the entrance hall is one of the most remarkable hotel lounges you're likely to see, with its series of bays formed by ancient rounded and pointed stone arches.

▶ Nearby

Rioja wine country To the north-east of Santa Domingo lies the broad valley of the Río Ebro, and the region around it known as La Rioja (after Santo Domingo's Río Oja, which flows into the Ebro at

Haro). It produces what is traditionally the best red wine of Spain, and one of the great wines of the world (see the chapter on 'Bed and board'). But it is not a wine area like those of France, highly picturesque and highly geared to the business of entertaining passing tourists. By French standards the vineyards are dishevelled affairs, the vines sprawling this way and that even though they are planted in regular rows; the wine is mostly made in industrial-scale *bodegas* concentrated in a few centres; and although you can visit these establishments (and taste their products) you normally have to do so by arrangement, and may even need an introduction from a wine shipper. This is not to say that it is an unattractive region – far from it; whether you're a wine lover or not, the Rioja is well worth a visit.

The wine-producing area extends a long way down the Ebro valley into the cereal and fruit-growing region below Logroño, but all the finer wines come from the part of the valley above Logroño, going up to and beyond Haro. This small, attractive town is for most purposes the capital of the Rioja wine country, and several of the most important *bodegas* are here or hereabouts. For an astounding view over the Rioja country as a whole, go up to the Balcón de Rioja, just south of the Puerto Herrera on the road from Logroño to Vitoria; the rich green-and-gold valley of the Ebro is there laid out in front of you, stretching away to the high *sierras* in the hazy distance. The small hill-top town of Laguardia, back down the road towards Logroño, is another wine centre which is worth a visit: the massive walls which once protected its narrow old streets from attack now protect them from invasion by cars. There are several prehistoric

Vineyards in Rioja Alavesa

finds in the area, including the recently excavated bronze-age settlement of La Hoya and a couple of roadside dolmens. Logroño need not be avoided – it is a spacious and prosperous town, and has an extravagant Baroque cathedral – but is unlikely to detain you for long.

Upper Ebro valley NW, 70km or so by road. Above Miranda, the Ebro has a hard time of it, forcing its way down from the heights of the *cordillera* to the plains to the south. What must have been a spectacular river gorge has been turned into a spectacular lake by the building of a dam above Puentelarra: upstream of the dam, the road twists along the lakeside beneath cliff-faces, while opposite, across the water, mountains rear up in huge rugged staircases. Eventually, the ground rises to the point where lake is once again replaced by river, and a few miles further on is Frías.

Frías One of the delights of an area like Northern Spain is that there are still undiscovered delights to be found. You'll find your own, and Frías is one of ours. Not that it goes unmentioned in other guides – with patience you can usually track it down – but it rarely gets the attention it deserves. From the road following the Ebro, between Trespaderne and Quintana-Martin Galindez, turn south on an even more minor road. The first of the rewards of Frías soon comes into view – a splendid many-arched fortified bridge with its central gate-tower intact and its cobbles neatly restored; the road takes a newer bridge across the swift-flowing Ebro but you can walk across the old one. The village of Frías itself is clearly in view from here – perched on a massive and precipitous lump of rock, with its crenellated battlements looking completely impenetrable. The road winds up and into the back of the village, which almost in its entirety has been carefully and charmingly restored – without turning it into a tourist trap. Not surprisingly, the views from the battlements across the Ebro valley are marvellous.

▶ Where to stay

Parador Nacional de Santo Domingo £££ ☎ 941 340300 A new hotel has been built around the splendid vaulted hall of the old pilgrims' hospice, hard by the cathedral; sadly, the furnishings and service are both a bit ragged, and some of the rooms distinctly cramped by Parador standards. Still, it's hard to resist the appeal of the historic setting.

■ SOS DEL REY CATÓLICO

In an area peppered with dust-coloured hill-top villages (on the borders of Navarra and Aragon), Sos del Rey Católico looks from a distance much like any other; late in the year, its buildings can barely be distinguished from the brown hills behind it. Approaching from the (rather unlikely) direction of the minor road from Uncastillo, it has a more individual look, thanks to the tall, square castle tower. But the real claims on the attention of the tourist are not obvious. One (and the more important for most visitors) is that perched on the north-west edge of the village is a better-than average Parador, new but stylishly built in a sympathetic fashion. The other is that this is the birthplace of Ferdinand of Aragon – or Ferdinand the Catholic – who first ruled a united Spain.

It is a calm, solid stone village, pleasant enough to wander around spotting the coats of arms on palace walls but without spectacular highlights (and with some danger of getting lost); that it has been designated a national historic and artistic monument is more a reflection of Ferdinand's achievements than anything else – and although there is clearly a lot of work going into tidying it up to meet tourist expectations, the main result for the moment is that there are countless building sites around the place, making it feel a bit like a half-built open-air museum. Go there with no greater expectation than a pleasant night or two in the Parador, and treat any other rewards as a bonus.

▶ What to see

San Esteban The church has a finely carved Romanesque doorway, and inside (if you can track down the key) you'll find interesting sculpted choir stalls.

▶ Nearby

Sangüesa NW, 15km by road. The appearance and odour of this small town are nowadays sadly dominated by industry, but it contains some interesting buildings dating from its medieval heyday. Chief among them is the transitional church of Santa Maria la Real, just by the bridge over the Aragon; it has an unusual and fine octagonal tower, and an elaborately sculptured south doorway which contains enough to entertain the dedicated student for hours: it depicts Biblical figures, craftsmen, the Last Judgement – even a Norse saga, apparently dictated by passing pilgrims.

Sierra de Leyre N, 40km or so by road. This half-day tour combines some very worthwhile sightseeing with scenic interest of every kind, from quiet vineyards to dramatic mountain gorges. It can be undertaken with a little more travelling from either Pamplona or Olite. The tour is described here in a clockwise fashion, but works equally well the other way.

From Sangüesa go north for Pamplona, joining the main N240 road near Liedena. On your right, across the valley of the Irati, is the apparently impenetrable wall of the Sierra de Leyre; but a mile or so up the road the wall is breached by a huge gash, the Hoz de Lumbier, cut through the mountains by the river. Reconstruction of the N240 made viewing of the defile tricky in 1985, but presumably parking arrangements will be restored in future. (For a closer inspection of the gorge, you can take a minor road either from Lumbier or from Liedena.)

At a crossroads a couple of miles further on, take the road for Lumbier; in about 15km, as you begin to descend from the high, wooded sierra, an even deeper defile opens up on your right, the Hoz de Arbayún. There is a car park and viewing platform – watch for signs – from which you can see right down into the precipitous canyon, hundreds of feet below. Huge birds circle overhead.

A couple of km further on you have a choice of route to Salvatierra – a continuation of the same good road, via Navascues and Burgui, or a more direct route via Biguewizal and Castello Nuevo on a single-track road which is not for the impatient. From Salvatierra the road cuts south through the Sierra de Orba via yet another defile – not dramatic enough to warrant designation as a Hoz – to the upper end of the Yesa reservoir. This big man-made lake is a popular place for watersports, at least in the early part of the summer when it can be expected to be full; later on, the level may have dropped to the point where the upper end presents views which are interesting rather than picturesque – expanses of grey earth, with the remains of drowned trees poking out.

Whatever the water-level, the valley is lent a dramatic air by the high, craggy lip of the Sierra de Leyre running its length on the northern side. On the slopes below the crags, but still high enough to give fine views over the valley, is the remarkable Monasterio de Leyre. The entrance doorway of the church has a finely carved surround, and the interior is harmonious and simple – particularly the original Romanesque part behind the altar. But it is the crypt underneath that part (entered via a small doorway at the other end of the monastery) which is really special – massive stone vaulting with simple, elegant carving which has an almost hieroglyphic quality. The monastery is still functioning, these days as a small hotel as well as a religious house (see 'Where to stay').

Uncastillo SE, 22km by road. A narrow road winds away into the hills from Sos del Rey Católico, first through terraced patches of wheatfield and then on to higher ground newly planted with pines, where there are fine views of the Pyrenees, far off to the north-east. As you drop down again, you need no help in identifying Uncastillo: the castillo itself is very prominent on a rocky outcrop above the roofs of the village. As you get closer, what catches the eye is not the castle but the towers of two of the churches, both of which have unusual turrets, Disney-style. At the far end of the village (with parking space in front) is Santa Maria; its south doorway is the

Santa Maria, Uncastillo

highlight, decorated in weird and wonderful ways – but don't miss the west front, with its bizarre group picture in relief above the door. If you follow narrow alleys up into the village, past sturdy houses of mellow stone, you'll eventually come to San Martin, the exterior of which is being restored. Climbing past it on the way to the castle, notice how the castle tower looks from below like a Hollywood façade, with no depth.

▶ Where to stay

Parador Nacional Fernando de Aragon ££ ☎ 948 888011 Built in the late 70s, this is one of the best modern Paradores, with traditional materials used in abundance – the floors throughout are of rough red tile. There is a spacious and stylish lobby, plus a rather more routine lounge on the fourth floor next to the coffee bar and restaurant – an attractive, spacious room with heavy arches of pale stone, and a shady outdoor terrace with wide views across the plain to the north-west. The bedrooms are not in any way extravagant, but more than adequate, and many have the same wide views over the plain. The food is prepared with more enthusiasm than is normal in Paradors.

Alternatives If you really want to get away from it all, you can stay at the Hospedería (£ ☎ 948 884100) run by the monks at the Monasterio de Leyre (see 'What to see'). It is simple but stylish and – as you might expect – very, very peaceful; it's also very good value.

■ VITORIA

Vitoria sits towards the western end of the high, prosperous plain of Alava, which is all but encircled by wooded mountains. The city is not in itself a remarkable place from the tourist's point of view, but it is well placed for trips in all directions into the surrounding mountains, and it is a more attractive place than most cities of its considerable size. The local Parador is right out in the country, a few miles along a good main road to the east.

The old centre of the city is unusually laid out, the narrow streets following oval contours around a long hill, with staircases linking one street to another in the steeper parts. One explanation of the name Vitoria is that the Basque word for a height is *beturia*; another is that it is a corruption of *victoria*, meaning (surprise, surprise) victory – and that it got this name when Sancho VI of Navarra defeated the Basques here in 1181. There seems to be agreement that its earlier name of Gasteiz (still shown as an alternative on some maps) is of Visigoth origin; about time it was dropped, you might think.

The modern city centre is spacious and prosperous, and many of its streets have rows of tall houses with the glazed balconies characteristic of Northern Spain.

► What to see

Old town None of the sights of the old town is individually remarkable, but a tour of the whole makes an interesting short walk – the old concentric streets contain many old houses and palaces. At the south end of the hill, and more-or-less at the focal point of the city as a whole, are the linked open spaces of the Plaza del Virgen Blanca and the arcaded Plaza de España in front of the Ayuntamiento; above them, the church of San Miguel, with a jolly polychromed statue of the Virgen Blanca (the city's patron saint) in the porch. Going clockwise around the hill and sticking to its lower levels, you come to the church of San Pedro, with a fine Gothic doorway. Steps lead up from here to the Correría, one of the main concentric streets; following this northward brings you to the Casa del Portalón, a restored timbered house with overhanging upper storeys. Just beyond it, built in much the same style, is the archaeological department of the Provincial Museum. Turning back to go down the eastern side of the hill, you come first to the fortress-like bulk of the old cathedral of Santa Maria; its most interesting feature is an ornate 14th-century doorway. The Chuchilleria, running south along the eastern slope of the hill, takes you past fine old houses now in a sorry state of repair – the Palacio de Bendaña and the Casa del Cordón – on your way back to your starting point.

Plaza del Virgen Blanca

▶ Nearby

Rioja wine country The places described under Santo Domingo can be reached from Vitoria with no great fuss – and approaching the Ebro valley from the north has the advantage that your first sight of the expanse of Rioja Alta will be the huge vista revealed as you cross the Sierra de Cantabria.

Sierra de Urbasa, Sierra de Andia, Estella See Pamplona.

Nervion valley The Nervion isn't one of Spain's great rivers – it runs only 40 miles or so from its beginning north-west of Vitoria to its meeting with the sea; but it has managed to provide Bilbao with the natural resources necessary to become a great seaport, and it has managed to carve out a valley of great splendour, at least in its upper reaches. The road from Vitoria to Orduña offers no great rewards until it reaches the lip of the valley, when a positive canyon opens up before you. In fact, the valley sides are in general not steep, but the high table-land either side ends in a distinct cliff which runs like a rim along the top of the slopes. By going down to Orduña and taking the tortuous road south, you can go via the Puerto de Orduña (again, splendid views) to the upper Ebro valley (see under Santo Domingo).

Estíbaliz E, 5 km by road. This hilltop monastery has a splendidly restored little Romanesque church which is a place of pilgrimage for the people of Alava – it contains a much venerated statue of the Virgin Mary, the patron saint of the province. The church is simplicity itself, apart from beautifully carved capitals and a handsome decorated south doorway.

Salvatierra E, 25km by road. Only a few miles beyond Argómaniz (see 'Where to stay'), this little town has a charming main street of balconied old houses and an arcaded central square.

Puerto de Urquiola N, 30km by road. A minor road leaving the the N240 at Villareal takes you on a gentle climb through attractively pastoral countryside to the pass, and then much more steeply down through rugged scenery towards Durango.

▶ Where to stay

Parador Nacional de Argómaniz ££ ☎ 945 282200 More than most Paradores, this one combines old and new. The old part is a solid stone palace which contains the public rooms – the dining room at the top, amid the roof beams, with the windows curiously at knee height. The bedrooms are in long wings running off from this central block, those at the front enjoying good views westward across the plains from their glazed balconies. In sum, it's not the kind of Parador to go out of your way for, but is nonetheless a restful place to pause.

Alternatives The main alternatives to the Parador are the upmarket hotels on the inner ring road of Vitoria, just south or west of the centre. Best in town is the four-star Gasteiz (£££ ☎ 945 228100), a glossy but tasteful modern block. The Canciller Ayala (£££ ☎ 945 220800) is by comparison distinctly dated in its décor, though it perhaps has a better position – opposite the Florida gardens, and with a bit of leafy park at the side. The General Alava (££ ☎ 945 222200) is a competent but unremarkable modern block, traditional and neat in its furnishing, offering good value.

PLANNING YOUR TRIP

How to get there, when to go, where to find out more

There are four main ways of getting there, assuming that you want the use of a car while you're there: taking your own car by ferry from Plymouth to Santander, by road through France, or by Motorail (putting the car on the train); or by going on a fly-drive deal, which gives you a flight and the use of a hire car while you're there. There's also an attractive hybrid way, which is to drive one way and take the boat the other.

When deciding on the timing of your trip you'll want to bear in mind variations in prices from one season to another – and the section on getting there gives some idea of how big these variations can be. But the main things to consider (apart from commitments at home) are the festivals and other events you might want to catch (or avoid), and the weather; these two factors are dealt with here in separate chapters.

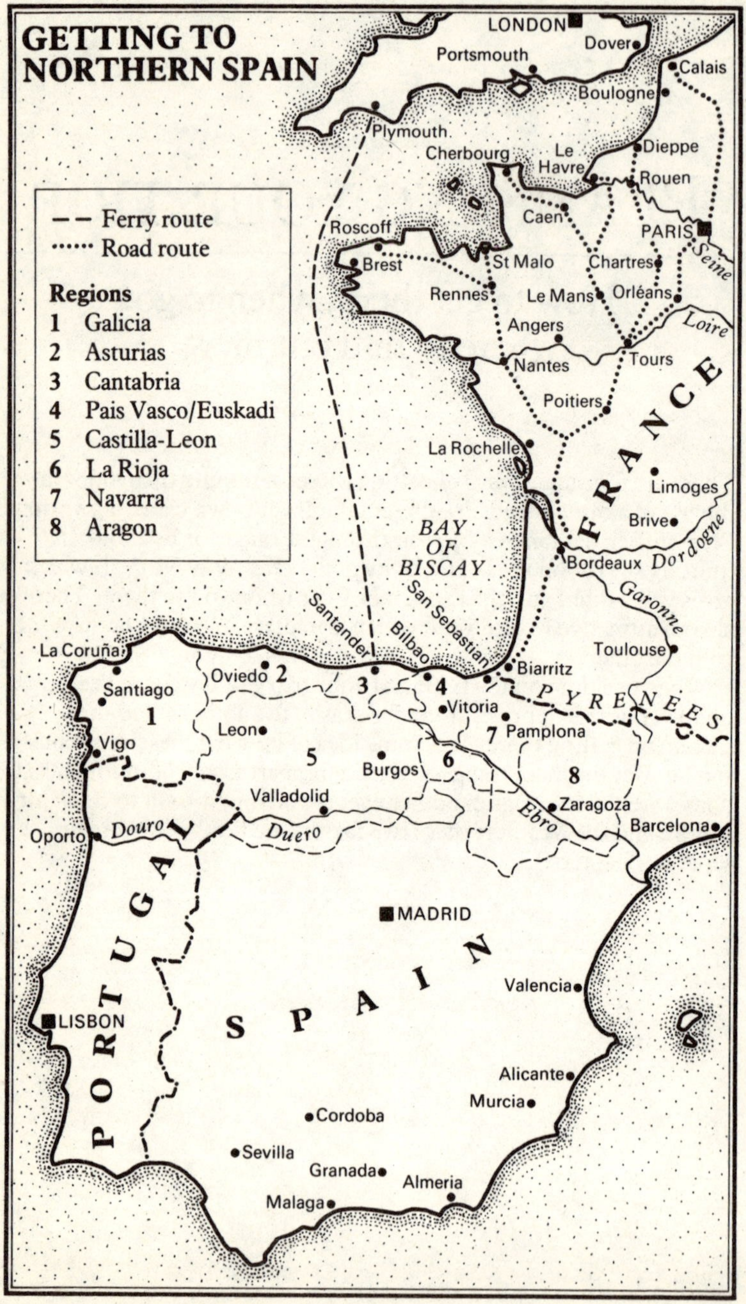
GETTING TO NORTHERN SPAIN
Ferry route
Road route
Regions
1 Galicia
2 Asturias
3 Cantabria
4 Pais Vasco/Euskadi
5 Castilla-Leon
6 La Rioja
7 Navarra
8 Aragon
LONDON
Dover
Portsmouth
Calais
Boulogne
Plymouth
Cherbourg
Le Havre
Dieppe
Rouen
Caen
PARIS
Seine
Roscoff
Brest
St Malo
Rennes
Chartres
Le Mans
Orléans
Loire
Angers
Nantes
Tours
Poitiers
FRANCE
La Rochelle
Limoges
Brive
BAY OF BISCAY
Bordeaux
Dordogne
Garonne
Santander
Bilbao
San Sebastian
Toulouse
Biarritz
PYRENEES
La Coruña
Oviedo
Santiago
Vitoria
Pamplona
Leon
Vigo
Burgos
Zaragoza
Ebro
Valladolid
Barcelona
Oporto
Douro
Duero
PORTUGAL
MADRID
SPAIN
Valencia
LISBON
Alicante
Murcia
Cordoba
Sevilla
Granada
Almeria
Malaga

HOW TO GET THERE

Going by boat

Brittany Ferries operate car ferries twice a week direct to Santander from Plymouth. The trip takes 24 hours, and the boat leaves Plymouth in the morning (the exact time varies throughout the year).

If the longest voyage you've made before is a one-hour Channel crossing, 24 hours may sound a long time to be at sea – particularly since over half that time is spent crossing the much-feared Bay of Biscay. After all, anyone who knows the slightest thing about sea-going matters can tell you with great authority that the Bay of Biscay is one of the world's most turbulent stretches of ocean. Its very name is practically synonymous with seasickness.

Over the centuries the Bay has certainly attracted a good deal of adverse comment. Leigh Hunt in his autobiography wrote of being becalmed in the Bay of Biscay: 'A calm in the Bay of Biscay, after what we had read and heard of it, sounded to us like a repose in a boiling cauldron.' H N Coleridge, author of 'Six Months in the West Indies', written at the beginning of the last century, found the Bay in a rather less forgiving mood: 'Have you ever been in a gale of wind off the Bay of Biscay? If not and you are fond of variety, it is really worth your while to take a trip to Lisbon or Madeira for the chance of meeting with one. Calculate your season well in December or January, when the south-wester has properly set in, and you will find it one of the finest and most uncomfortable things in the world. *My* gale lasted from Sunday till Wednesday evening, which is something long, perhaps, for amusement, but it gave ample scope for observation and philosophy.' A remark attributed to Andrew Cherry captures the opinion of many sufferers of *mal de mer*: 'In the Bay of Biscay, O!'.

But is the Bay of Biscay really as black as it's painted? Certainly it can be rough – but then so can most large stretches of water. And those who travel across it regularly say that it is no more likely to be stormy than the English Channel or the North Sea. So why has it had such a bad press?

It seems likely that it earned its bad reputation with the early English mariners – such as Drake and Hawkins – who set sail from the south-west coast in the 16th century. The first stretch of very deep water they encountered was beyond the north-west tip of

Brittany at the start of the Bay of Biscay where the European continental shelf ends and the sea bottom suddenly drops away from a depth of around 400 feet to the ocean depths of over two miles. For these ancient mariners, in their tiny sailing boats, this deep water and its turbulence in bad weather must have been truly alarming. For the modern-day car-ferry passenger, in a large, stabilised ship, the Bay of Biscay should present no great terrors. During the summer you would be unlucky to encounter a serious storm; on our various research trips we failed to glimpse even so much as a white horse. (For those who believe in being prepared, there's advice on preventing and dealing with seasickness in 'Background facts' on page 153.)

In good weather, the 24-hour sailing can even be enjoyable, provided you're in a relaxed frame of mind and you're not short of reading matter or conversational companions. About seven hours out from Plymouth, the ferry rounds the coast of Brittany, passing Brest and the Pointe du Raz. The ship has to steer a careful course between a number of islands and rocky outcrops, passing surprisingly close to shore and offering views of sandy beaches and white-washed Breton houses. As you travel south, the sun gets stronger and (provided you're out of the wind), you can do some serious sunbathing even before you've arrived in Spain. The climax of the journey is, of course, the arrival in Santander. When you arrive in the morning, it's worth making the effort to get up on deck a bit early in time to catch a first exciting glimpse of Northern Spain: the town of Santander, no more than a grey smudge on the horizon, dwarfed by the huge mountains that rear up behind it.

The ferry crossing offers other attractions; good food – particularly at the excellent value eat-as-much-as-you-like buffet restaurant. There is also a cinema showing recently released movies (there is a charge, but it's still very popular – get there early to be sure of a seat) and a play room for the children – as well as a duty- and tax-free shop. But when the sun is shining, you will simply want to sit out on deck in an easy chair and relax. Quite a few people find the voyage so attractive that they happily take Brittany Ferries' 'mini-cruises', travelling out and straight back with just a few hours ashore in Santander.

The cost In 1987, a return crossing for two adults and a car up to 4 metres in length works out at £508 in high season and £380 in low season, including cabin accommodation. Not cheap, but certainly good value – it works out at around a tenth of the cost per mile of the short Channel crossings. It also works out as reasonably good value when you compare the fare with the cost of driving down and back to Northern Spain through France: a return Channel fare, with the added cost of overnight accommodation, autoroute charges, petrol and wear-and-tear on your car (see the next section). (There is a reduced ferry fare for a car and two adults staying less than eight days.)

Driving through France

St Malo is the nearest Channel port to Spain – from there to the French-Spanish border is a journey of around 640km (400 miles). The drive is a fairly easy one – the only problem area is Nantes, where, in true Gallic style, vital signposts are missing at important junctions. From Nantes the road continues through pleasant country to Niort, where there is a motorway to take you most of the way to Spain, skirting Saintes, Bordeaux and Biarritz.

The drive can be done very quickly if you're keen to get there. Leaving St Malo at 8.30am, by driving steadily but not frantically – and with a couple of stops en route – we reached the Spanish border at 6.30pm. But it would be a pity to drive down through France and not see some of the exquisite countryside to be discovered off the *autoroute*. The most promising opportunities for diversions are south of Nantes, where you could choose to linger in the charming Marais Poitevin district, which has been described as a 'Green Venice'. It's a region of delightful canals which pass through picturesque little villages; every pasture is practically an island – nearly everything has to be moved around in flat-bottomed boats.

This is Poitou-Charentes, one of the most delightful areas of France, with dozens of fascinating towns and cities to explore. You should certainly take a look at Aulnay, which was an important stopping point for pilgrims en route to Santiago de Compostela (known to the French as St Jacques de Compostelle); since you will also probably be including Santiago in your itinerary, it will be a fitting place to stop. The Romanesque church there has some marvellous sculptures. (Other key points on the French part of the Pilgrims' Way were Saintes, Pons and St-Jean-Pied-de-Port, where the three pilgrims' roads from Le Puy, Paris and Vézelay met.)

Further south is Cognac, the home of brandy; and the major wine-producing areas of the Bordeaux region. Among the châteaux you can visit are those at Médoc, particularly Margaux and Mouton-Rothschild, and also Graves. Perhaps the most attractive spot is St Emilion. You could easily linger on your journey several days in this area of France, which continues to be one of the most popular with British travellers.

You should also try to include a stop in the Gascon region south-west of Bordeaux, and visit some of the marvellous places to be found among the man-made pine forests of the Landes. Near

Mimizan there are a number of splendid small lakes (*étangs* in French) among the sweet-smelling pine forests. The nearby coast has a beach which runs almost the whole 150km length of the Landes, swept by huge Atlantic breakers: a spectacular sight and sound on a windy day.

Almost on the Spanish border are the stylish resorts of Biarritz and the smaller St-Jean-de-Luz, which are both charming, unspoilt seaside towns.

The cost If you're going to make proper comparisons between the cost of driving to Northern Spain and the alternative ways of getting there, you've got to take more into account than just the petrol used in driving 400 miles in each direction – even if you don't make use of French motorways (which carry substantial tolls), you ought to make some allowance for wear and tear on your car. It's very likely that you'll want to stop for at least one night on each leg of the journey; whether that should properly be counted as part of the cost of getting there is debatable, since you could equally well count it as an extension of the holiday. But assuming you *do* count in a night's accommodation the total for two adults works out at about £120 on top of the return ferry fare, which for Portsmouth–St Malo in 1987 ranges from £218 to £308 (including a cabin). The shorter Channel crossings, from Dover for example, cost less but leave you with quite a bit further to drive.

D.O.S.H. (Drive Out, Ship Home)

As an alternative to taking the Plymouth-Santander ferry in both directions (or driving in both directions), you might consider driving down through France to Northern Spain and taking the ferry back. (It will make more sense to do things this way round, rather than going out on the boat, because after a couple of weeks driving round Northern Spain you probably won't feel much like driving home through France. One of the great treats after a couple of weeks in Northern Spain is getting on the ferry at Santander to enjoy a cup of tea and yesterday's edition of the *Daily Telegraph*!)

The cost Except in the peak months of July and August, Brittany Ferries has a 'cruise and drive' package which includes a Channel crossing (to either Roscoff or St Malo), a return sailing from Santander to Plymouth (the journey can be done the other way around for a small supplement) and hotel accommodation en route in France and Spain for either 5, 7, 11 or 14 nights. A 14-night package in June or September for two adults sharing a room costs £418 per person in 1987, including a cabin. You can of course organise your own accommodation and simply buy tickets for the two ferries: a one-way Portsmouth–St Malo crossing with a car and two-berth cabin costs £157 on peak-fare sailings, £109 in low season or on unpopular sailings; a one-way Santander–Plymouth crossing with a two-berth cabin costs £274 in high season, £190 in low season.

Motorail

If you want to take your own car but don't want to take the ferry to Santander or to drive down through France, you could take it on the train with the French equivalent of Motorail. In summer there is a weekly service (on Tuesday nights in 1987) from Boulogne to Biarritz near the Spanish border, and there are more frequent year-round services from Paris. If you're interested in visiting the eastern part of the area, and if you live close to the Channel ports of Dover or Folkestone, this is likely to be the most convenient way of getting to Northern Spain. If you live north or west of London, and if your real interest lies in the western part of the area, it can mean a lot of driving even though you've cut out most of France.

The cost The second class return fare from Boulogne to Biarritz for two adults and a car, including the applicable cross-Channel ferry rate from Dover or Folkestone, together with a two-bed sleeper, is £495 in 1987.

Fly-drive

You don't have to take your own car to have a motoring holiday: you can fly out and use a hired car. There are direct flights from London to Bilbao in the eastern part of the area – operated by both British Airways (from Gatwick) and Iberia (from Heathrow) – and to Santiago in the west, operated by Iberia; at either airport you can have a hired car ready to collect on arrival. The attractions of fly-drive are that you get to your destination quickly (110 minutes flying time to Santiago from Heathrow), and that you have a left-hand-drive car, better suited to driving on Continental roads. The problems of sorting out insurance, bail bonds, red warning triangles and the rest are the responsibility of the car hire company – all you have to do is collect the car and drive off.

The main disadvantage of flying is that you are heavily restricted in the amount of luggage you can take with you – and whatever you take has to be lugged through two airports twice. On a driving holiday in Northern Spain, you are likely to want to take a substantial amount of equipment with you. Given the varying types of weather you can expect to encounter, you will probably find it helpful to have a choice of clothes and coats. Taking your own car, you can toss in a selection of things which may or may not prove to be absolutely indispensable (everything from a Swiss Army penknife and a packet of Bran Buds to Michelin maps and guides, a gas stove and a kettle) – articles which space and weight restrictions will prevent you from taking if you fly. If you have children, especially young children, the quantity of extra kit you'll want to take (nappies, pushchairs, babyfood etc) will probably make flying an impractical alternative.

Going one step further, you can buy a complete holiday based on the fly-drive idea – from Mundi-Color or Travelscene, for example. For most people, the principal attraction of a fly-drive package is that it is completely undemanding: all hotels are pre-booked, so that you have a ready-made itinerary to follow from the moment you arrive. (On a number of the Brittany Ferries deals, you just have the first couple of nights booked for you – for the rest of your stay, you book hotels as you go along.) But with a completely pre-booked itinerary you have no flexibility to linger at places that are particularly appealing, or to pass by establishments that prove to be less congenial than you might have expected. Pay your money and take your choice.

The cost For those who want to sort out their own hotel arrangements, Iberia offer a return flight to Bilbao or Santiago, with seven nights' car hire; in 1986 this sort of deal cost around £415 for two people during high season.

Mundi-Color offer a couple of complete fly-drive packages which include Northern Spain. For example, in 1986 a 12-night 'Paradores of Galicia' package – including accommodation (room and breakfast only) in Santiago de Compostela, Verín, Bayona and Cambados – cost around £600 per person during the high season, £550 in low season.

Travelscene offer packages including flight from Heathrow to Bilbao and seven nights' accommodation in Paradores at Santillana del Mar, Fuente Dé, Cervera de Pisuerga, Santo Domingo de la Calzada and Argómaniz. The cost in 1986 was around £340 in high season, £270 in low season.

■ WEATHER

Northern Spain is often referred to as the 'wet' coast of Spain; with a northern shore facing the notorious Bay of Biscay, and its western side exposed to the full force of the Atlantic Ocean, it shouldn't be surprising that the climate of the north is generally less favourable than that of the Mediterranean south. But for visitors from Britain the climate isn't at all unattractive – in general it's warmer and sunnier than Britain, even if most parts are also wetter. If you're planning a touring holiday, the weather will probably suit you fine; if you're intending to spend all your time on the beach, there are undoubtedly holiday areas which are less likely to disappoint you.

If you're bothered about the weather it's important to study it in some detail, because there are pronounced variations from one place to another. Don't assume that just because one city is 100 or more miles from another, you can expect similar weather in each. The most striking example of this is the two-hour drive from Oviedo to León, which takes you over the mountains. Frequently, the weather in Oviedo can be dull and cloudy while on the other side of the mountains León is basking in cloudless heat.

Budding statisticians will find plenty to keep them busy in the tables which follow, where we compare the temperature, rainfall and sunshine averages for seven places in Northern Spain with those for Barcelona (at the northern end of Spain's Mediterranean coast) and London. But ordinary mortals will probably welcome a guided tour of the weather scene.

The picture changes a lot from one season of the year to another. In spring, daytime temperatures tend to be much the same across the whole area, and a few degrees higher than in Britain – on average climbing each day to about 16°C compared with 13°C in London. Inland places get about as much rain as London, and coastal places (plus Pamplona, of the places in our tables) distinctly more. On the other hand, it's sunnier than London – particularly inland, but to an appreciable extent everywhere.

Summer temperatures on the coasts are only slightly higher than in London, but there are much higher temperatures inland – almost on a par with those in Barcelona. The amount of rain varies widely, with Gijón and Santander on the north coast getting slightly more than London (except in July) while the cities of Burgos and León get very much less – León, in particular, gets very little in July and August. The north coast barely does better than London for sunshine, either, while westerly places get considerably more and inland places are sunny for almost eighty per cent of the time.

While England cools down rapidly in the autumn, Northern Spain stays warm for much longer, especially on the coast – in October and November, you can expect coastal temperatures to climb a full five degrees higher than in London, and even those inland may be a little higher. The sunshine record, too, is much better than at home. But as winter approaches the amount of rain falling increases in coastal places to two or three times what we expect in London. In the depth of winter, the summer roles are reversed and its the inland places which are cooler than the coastal ones – though still warmer than Britain.

The mountains, of course, play an important part in influencing the weather, and this is particularly obvious in the winter and spring when there are heavy snow-falls. In mid-May, for example, we found ourselves briefly stranded in the Parador at Fuente Dé, in the heart of the Picos de Europa, by a severe snow storm. An hour's drive away, down in the valley, the sun was shining brightly.

In the weather charts on the next page, for selected towns and for each month of the year, we have listed the average daily maximum temperature, the average total monthly rainfall and the average amount of sunshine (expressed as a percentage of the number of hours it's possible for the sun to shine).

▶ How cold it gets at night, on average (°C)

	Jan	Feb	Mar	Apr	May	Jun	Jul	Aug	Sep	Oct	Nov	Dec
Burgos	-1	0	2	4	7	10	12	12	11	7	3	1
Fisterra	8	7	9	10	11	13	15	15	15	13	11	9
Gijón	6	6	8	9	11	14	16	16	15	12	9	7
La Coruña	7	7	8	9	11	13	15	15	14	12	9	8
León	-1	-1	2	4	6	10	12	12	10	6	2	0
Pamplona	1	1	4	6	9	12	14	14	12	8	4	2
Santander	7	7	8	10	11	14	16	16	15	12	10	8
Barcelona	6	7	9	11	14	18	21	21	19	15	11	8
London	2	2	3	6	8	12	14	13	11	8	5	4

▶ How warm it gets in the day, on average (°C)

	Jan	Feb	Mar	Apr	May	Jun	Jul	Aug	Sep	Oct	Nov	Dec
Burgos	6	8	12	15	18	22	26	25	22	16	10	7
Fisterra	12	13	15	16	18	20	22	23	21	19	15	13
Gijón	13	13	15	16	17	20	23	23	21	19	15	13
La Coruña	13	13	15	16	18	20	22	23	22	19	15	13
León	7	9	13	16	19	24	28	27	23	18	12	7
Pamplona	8	10	14	16	20	24	27	27	24	19	13	9
Santander	12	12	14	15	17	20	22	22	21	18	15	13
Barcelona	13	14	16	18	21	25	28	28	25	21	16	13
London	6	7	10	13	17	20	22	21	19	14	10	7

▶ How much rain falls, in total (mm)

	Jan	Feb	Mar	Apr	May	Jun	Jul	Aug	Sep	Oct	Nov	Dec
Burgos	48	39	53	47	59	52	28	27	46	54	50	57
Fisterra	96	67	92	51	55	38	19	41	57	76	127	124
Gijón	114	93	75	75	93	59	42	68	75	105	108	127
La Coruña	118	80	92	67	54	45	28	46	61	87	124	135
León	57	41	61	43	53	39	17	16	39	48	55	65
Pamplona	120	86	79	83	90	84	46	44	67	107	107	140
Santander	119	88	78	83	89	63	54	84	114	133	125	159
Barcelona	31	39	48	43	54	37	27	49	76	86	52	45
London	54	40	37	37	46	45	57	59	49	57	64	48

▶ How much the sun shines (% of possible hours)

	Jan	Feb	Mar	Apr	May	Jun	Jul	Aug	Sep	Oct	Nov	Dec
Burgos	27	42	45	56	58	62	78	74	61	49	36	25
Fisterra	31	36	37	51	50	53	57	57	49	51	39	29
Gijón	29	37	38	42	39	38	42	48	37	39	32	27
La Coruña	34	42	38	49	49	49	56	57	47	45	39	30
León	50	53	50	64	58	64	80	78	63	54	47	38
Pamplona	25	37	37	45	43	52	65	62	52	45	33	22
Santander	29	37	41	43	42	42	44	45	41	40	33	26
Barcelona	53	55	48	55	56	62	68	67	53	49	48	44
London	18	23	31	38	41	43	39	41	37	30	20	16

FIESTAS

Spain is a country that has a passion for public celebrations; almost every day of the year seems to be a fiesta day somewhere in the country. While we British for the most part get fearfully embarrassed and self-conscious about the business of dressing up in strange costumes and parading around the streets with a smile on our faces, for the Spanish it seems to be an intrinsic part of their everyday life. Their pageants are not the product of endless committee meetings of the local Round Table, but clearly a more spontaneous re-enactment of a civic tradition that dates back hundreds of years. In many cases, the reasons for doing what they're doing are no longer known – but nobody cares very much, the celebration is enough for itself.

The people of Northern Spain are particularly keen on fiestas. It's well worth organising your itinerary, if you can, to include a fiesta or two on your journey. To be caught up in the excitement of a town's festivities is an experience to remember. The fiesta that's best-known outside Spain, thanks largely to the writings of Ernest Hemingway, is the San Fermin festival held in Pamplona every July – see page 113. Less violent and perhaps rather more to your taste will be one of the many fiestas in smaller towns organised for local consumption rather than the enjoyment of tourists. Fiestas such as the 'A Rapa das Bestas' held every July in the Galician towns of Vivero and San Lorenzo, where wild horses are brought into town to have their manes and tails clipped – and for the colts to be branded. The wild horses are raced around the town, and then released on the mountains. All visitors are treated to a steaming bowl of garlic soup.

Below is a guide to the main fiestas of Northern Spain, with the dates for 1987. Before you book your holiday, check with the Spanish National Tourist Office in London to confirm these dates.

* means exact date not known at time of publication

Easter

Valladolid April 12–19
Holy Week Major religious processions throughout Holy Week, reaching a climax at noon on Good Friday in the Plaza Mayor.

Aviles, Oviedo province April 19–20
Bollo On Easter Sunday and Monday, the town holds a variety of

festivities including a parade of floats reviewed by the queen of the festival, an exhibition and competition of prize cattle; there are boat races on the river.

Pola de Siero, Oviedo province April 21
Painted eggs festival On Easter Tuesday, eggs are painted with coloured dyes and sold. There is a large folklore parade in the afternoon when groups which represent each of the Councils of Asturias parade through the town in typical dress and perform their regional dance as they pass in front of the town hall.

April

Ribadavia, Orense province *
Ribeiro wine exposition-fair Numerous ceremonies to celebrate the local wines, which are offered free to visitors together with local fruit; much local music, singing and dancing.

San Vicente de la Barquera, Santander province *
La Folia Festivities in honour of the Virgin patroness of the town which begin first thing in the morning with lively dawn songs (*alboradas*), continue with a parade and climax with the Procession of the Virgin – the statue is carried by sailors to an altar on the dockside, where local dances are performed.

May

Corvera de Asturias, Oviedo province May 3
Tour of the Trasona Dam Asturian folk celebrations, a contest between wooden shoe makers and artisans, also sports events.

Santo Domingo de la Calzada, La Rioja province May 10–15
Patron Saint festivals Celebrations begin with the Parade of the Rams: two rams adorned with regional decorations which will be sacrificed for the saint's dinner. There is also a procession of oak branches and a procession of prioresses.

Miranda de Ebro, Burgos province June 8
Celebration of San Juan del Monte On Whit Monday there is a long procession of groups of people wearing bright blouses and coloured neckerchiefs, and carrying musical instruments. On their way through the town they sing, dance and wave their berets. There is also a drive to the sanctuary of the saint in beautifully decorated carriages.

Puenteareas, Pontevedra province June 17–18
Corpus Christi Carpets of flowers are laid out on the streets along the path of the Eucharist.

June

Castrillo de Murcia, Burgos province June 21
Colacho This is a fiesta whose origins lie in the pantomimes and games of the Roman theatre, which were subsequently adapted into Middle Age mystery plays. The fiesta is dominated by the figure of Colacho, who represents Evil.

Castro Urdiales, Santander province Last week in June
Coso Blanco A battle of flowers, a firework display and a night parade of coaches.

Cudillero, Oviedo province June 29
La Amuravela An effigy of San Pedro is carried out to sea, where a poem, partly religious but partly mocking, is read out giving an account of what has happened in the previous year.

Haro, La Rioja province June 29
Pilgrimage of San Felices de Bilibio The highlight is the Battle of Wine, where the men of the town squirt wine at each other from their wine bags.

Burgos June 28–July 5
The Day of Las Peñas The most important Burgos fiesta which includes among other things an international folklore festival. At Fuentes Blancas, 10km outside the city, there is also a competition to cook a specified dish and another of the contestant's own choosing.

Irún, Guipuzcoa province June 30
Alarde de San Marcial Twelve batallions, made up of 2,000 men with torch bearers and cavalry, march to the saint's hermitage on his feast day.

July

Burgos June 28–July 5
See above.

San Lorenzo de Sabucedo-La Estrada, Pontevedra province July 5
A Rapa des Bestas At dawn wild horses are brought from the mountains; they are then broken in by an *agarrador* and their manes are trimmed.

Vivero, Lugo province July 5
A Rapa das Bestas Similar to the above festivities but with races and free garlic soup.

Pamplona July 6–14
San Fermin The running of the bulls, bands of *txistularis* – Basque flute players and bagpipers – singing, dancing and drinking. One of Spain's most famous fiestas.

Pontevedra July 11
San Benitiño de Lerez The climax of the fiesta is a large outdoor lunch complete with bagpipes and Galician songs ending with choral concerts and local dancing.

Anguiano, La Rioja province July 21–23
The Dance of the Stilts Eight young men dance on stilts 40cm high to the music of bagpipes and drums (in celebration of the feast of St Mary Magdalen).

Cangas de Onis, Oviedo province July 25
Shepherd's Festival A fiesta to honour the shepherds of the Covadonga mountains; sports competitions, games and a song-and-dance contest.

Luarca, Oviedo province July 26
Vaqueiros de Alzada A fiesta for the cattle farmers from neighbouring valleys including traditional music and a 'cowherd's wedding'.

Estella, Navarra July 31–August 6
Patron Saint Festivals Brass bands, calf-running through the streets, solemn processions and an open-air feast.

August

Estella, Navarra July 31–August 6
See above.

Arriondas-Ribadesella, Oviedo province August 2
Asturias Canoe Race Festival Parade of canoe racers and the race itself.

Gijón August 2
Asturias Day The highlight is a spectacular and dramatic parade of decorated floats with regional and foreign folk groups.

Ribadeo, Lugo province August 2
Holy Cross Festival Famous for its regional music with contests between quartets and quintets of bagpipes.

Cambados, Pontevedra province August 2
Albariño Wine Festival Wine tasting, carousing and sports events.

Vitoria August 4–8
Festival of the White Virgin All sorts of goings-on, starting and finishing with fireworks; dawn procession, bullfights, clowns in the street.

Cabezon de la Sal, Santander province August 9
Mountain Day Contests of pipe players, tambourine and rebeck players; mountain songs, lassooing and tugs of war between cattle.

Foz, Lugo province August 10
San Lorenzo Festival Canoeing regattas, sports competitions as well as folk entertainment.

Betanzos, La Coruña province August 14–25
San Roque Festival Traditional dances of farmers and sailors; a battle of flowers and the launching of a huge balloon.

Sada, La Coruña province *
San Roque Festival Boat races, float parade, launching of a giant balloon and the serving of baked sardines with free wine.

Llanes, Oviedo province August 16
San Roque Festival People dressed in typical regional costumes, bagpipe music and children dancing.

Torrelavega, Santander province August 16
Floral gala Parade of floats decorated with flowers and folk music groups.

Vivero, Lugo province August 23
El Naseiro Romeiro A festival of Galician singing and dancing.

Laredo, Santander province August 28
Battle of Flowers Parades of floats.

Cadavedo-Luarca, Oviedo province August 30
Regalina Parade of decorated carts accompanied by pipers, drummers and local dance groups.

September

Tordesillas, Valladolid province September 15
Toro de la Vega Running of the bulls.

Logroño September 18–27
La Rioja grape harvest festival Treading of the grapes and the blessing and offering of the first wine must to the Virgen de Valvanera; parade of wagons and carriages as well as performances by Spanish and foreign folks groups and bands.

Oviedo *

America's Day Floats, bands, folk groups with a Latin American flavour.

Mieres, Oviedo province September 27

Pilgrimage of Saints Cosme and Damian Music and dancing; visitors are offered cider from the first harvest in Asturias.

Reinosa, Santander province September 27

Day of Campóo Bands, parades and contests, all in traditional regional dress.

October

El Grove, Pontevedra October 11

Marisco festival

Mondoñedo, Lugo province October 17

As San Lucas One of the most important fairs in north-east Spain for horse, mule and donkey sales. Singing, dancing and drinking.

BACKGROUND FACTS

A miscellaneous collection of useful information to help you avoid problems while you're in Northern Spain, arranged under headings in alphabetical order.

Currency During 1986 the value of the £ in pesetas declined by over 20 per cent; when the first edition of this guide was finalised, the peseta was worth just about one old penny – about 240 to the £; now, you get only 190 to the £. By the time you read this, of course, the rate could have changed again. Paradores and other tourist hotels will change currency, as will El Corte Inglés department stores.

Duty-free allowances Spain is now a member of the EEC, which means that the amounts of wine and other goods you are allowed to bring into Britain from Spain increased to match the amounts you may be used to bringing back from France. (Lower limits apply to any goods you buy in a duty-free shop on your way home, rather than in an ordinary shop in Spain.) Leaflets stating the current limits are freely available from travel agents and port offices; probably the most important figures to remember are those for alcohol. You're allowed a total of seven litres of wines and spirits per person, provided the spirits are not over 38.8° proof and don't amount to more than three of the seven litres.

Electrical supply Normally 220 volts (50 cycles AC), although sometimes you will find 125 volts only (and occasionally both voltages in the same hotel!); sockets are normally for two-pin plugs, but some have side-earth contacts of the kind used widely elsewhere on the Continent.

Health matters Opinions differ on the safety of drinking tap water: we drank it and survived intact, but some tour couriers, at least, advise against it. Now that Spain has joined the EEC, it has for the first time a reciprocal health care agreement with Britain; this means that British citizens are entitled to the same health care, at the same cost, as Spanish citizens. It does *not* mean that you no longer need insurance when visiting Spain; for a number of reasons which we don't have space to explain here, it still makes very good sense to buy a travel insurance package from your travel agent, ferry company, tour operator, insurance broker or insurance company.

Local time Spain is basically one hour ahead of Greenwich Mean Time; its summer time is two hours ahead of GMT – so Spain is normally one hour ahead of Britain. Up to now, clocks have been put back to winter time about a month sooner on the Continent than in Britain, so there has been a short period (in October) when time in the two countries has been the same. There are plans to bring the change-overs into line.

Maps Unless you are planning a very conservative itinerary, you will need more detailed road maps than those in this book. Several publishers produce maps of the whole of Spain at a scale of 1:1 million, which will suffice only if you are going to stick to major roads. The best (and the best value) has traditionally been Michelin sheet 990; but it has more competition in 1987 in the shape of the new Telegraph International Road Map series. There are two main series of more detailed maps to consider. Michelin cover all of Northern Spain in two sheets at a scale of 1:400,000 – 42 covers the eastern half, 441 the western half and northern Portugal. Firestone offer two main possibilities: at 1:500,000, sheets C-1 and C-2 cover the whole area, with a very large overlap in the middle; the T series (Tourist maps) at 1:200,000 would take six or more sheets to cover the whole area; they have detailed street plans of major towns and cities on the back. The Firestone R series (at a similar scale) is highly regarded but difficult to find in the shops.

Opening hours Traditionally, shops open late in the morning, close for the early afternoon and reopen again in the late afternoon, then staying open well into the evening; but shops in tourist centres increasingly tailor their opening times to suit the whims of visitors, and many big city-centre stores stay open all day until late evening. Banks are open only in the mornings (but are open on Saturdays as well as weekdays), though some exchange bureaux may reopen in the evening. Post offices generally follow banking hours, though some are also open in the early evening.

Public holidays There are more national public holidays in Spain than we're used to in Britain, and finding out exactly when to expect them isn't easy. The current tourist office list is as follows:
New Year's Day, Epiphany (6 January), St Joseph's Day (19 March), Maundy Thursday, Good Friday, Easter Monday (16, 17 and 20 April 1987), Labour Day (1 May), Corpus Christi (second Thursday after Whitsun – 18 June 1987), St James's Day (25 July), Assumption (15 August), All Saints' (1 November), Christmas Day. There are also local holidays for individual towns' feast days.

Public toilets Britain seems to be about the only country in the world that pays much attention to the need for public toilets. In Spain, expect to find relief only in your hotel or a restaurant or museum (look for 'los aseos' or 'los servicios').

Seasickness Medical advice is that prevention of seasickness is better than cure. If you're expecting trouble, the best plan is to lie down, or at least to sit down somewhere near the centre of the ship, where its motion will be less pronounced. When not lying down, try to keep your eyes on the horizon rather than on the deck of the ship or the boiling sea. Don't eat big meals, don't drink alcohol and don't smoke. There are drugs such as Phenergan and Dramamine which can help to prevent seasickness, but they are basically sedatives which serve to put you to sleep – the theory is that by the time you wake up you will have acquired your 'sea legs'. There's nothing wrong with this except for drivers, who will need their wits about them especially during the first few hours on the Continent and who should avoid anything likely to cause drowsiness.

Telephones Even in the remotest parts of Northern Spain you will find copious supplies of telephone boxes, which offer international direct dialling facilities – and are a lot cheaper than calling from your hotel room. To call the UK, dial 07, wait for a second tone, then dial 44 followed by the UK STD code, omitting the initial '0'.

World service If you want to keep in touch with the world while you're away, you can try tuning in to the BBC World Service on the short waveband; there are four possible frequencies /wavelengths: 12.09MHz/19.91m, 9.41MHz/31.88m, 7.185MHz/41.75m and 5.975MHz/50.21m. The lower frequencies (longer wavelengths) will normally give best results in the evening and early morning, the higher frequencies (shorter wavelengths) in the middle of the day.

■ MORE INFORMATION

Names, addresses and phone numbers you'll find helpful if you want to know more about travel to Northern Spain.

Car ferries

Brittany Ferries Millbay Docks, Plymouth PL1 3EW
☎ 0752 221321

Flights

British Airways ☎ 01-759 2525
Iberia ☎ 01-437 9822

Fly/drive packages

Mundi Color Holidays 276 Vauxhall Bridge Road, London SW1V 1BE ☎ 01-834 3492
Travelscene 94 Baker Street, London W1M 2HD
☎ 01-935 1025

Tourist information offices

Offices in Northern Spain:

Bilbao Alameda Mazarredo ☎ 94 4236430
Burgos Plaza de Alonso Martinez 7 ☎ 947 203125
Gijón Marqués de San Esteban 1 ☎ 985 846046
La Coruña Dársena de la Marina ☎ 981 221822
Laredo Lopez Seña ☎ 942 605492
León Plaza de Regla 4 ☎ 987 237082
Logroño Miguel Villanueva 11 ☎ 941 255497
Lugo Plaza de España 27-29 ☎ 982 231361
Orense Curros Enriquez 1 ☎ 988 234717
Oviedo Plaza de la Catedral 6 ☎ 985 346046
Pamplona Beloso Alto, Carretera Nacional 121 ☎ 948 249393
Ponferrada Avenida de la Puebla ☎ 987 415537
Pontevedra General Mola 1 ☎ 986 850814
San Sebastián Miramar esquina Andina ☎ 943 426282
Santander Plaza Porticada ☎ 942 310708

Santiago de Compostela Rua del Villar 43 ☎ 981 584081
Santillana del Mar Plaza Mayor ☎ 942 818251
Tuy Puente Trippes ☎ 986 601785
Vigo Jardines de Eldayen ☎ 986 430577
Vitoria Parque de la Florida ☎ 945 249564

National Tourist Offices in London:

Spanish National Tourist Office 57/58 St James's Street, London SW1A 1LD ☎ 01-499 0901
French Government Tourist Office 179 Piccadilly, London W1V 0AL ☎ 01-491 7622
Portuguese National Tourist Office 1-5 New Bond House, New Bond Street, London W1 ☎ 01-493 3873

Hotel booking

London booking service for Paradores:

Keytel International 402 Edgware Road, London W2 1ED ☎ 01-402 8182/3/4

HELP WITH FUTURE EDITIONS

We plan to revise *Spain's Hidden Country* regularly, to take account of the changes which are only to be expected in an area which is only beginning to realise its potential as a tourist destination. We should be grateful for your help in this task, and the form set out over these two pages is designed to make it easy for you to give us the sort of information we need; photocopy this double-page spread if you like, and write directly on the copy – or simply use our headings to set out your report on a blank piece of paper.

Hotels

Tell us about the ones you liked and the ones you disliked: name them, and say *why* you feel the way you do

RECOMMENDED

NOT RECOMMENDED

Restaurants

In later editions we'll be aiming to extend the coverage of restaurants in this book; again, pick out the good and the bad, and say *why*

RECOMMENDED

NOT RECOMMENDED

Sights

What were the real 'finds' of your holiday – whether man-made or natural? And what were the disappointments?

RECOMMENDED

NOT RECOMMENDED

▶ INDEX